SPIRITUAL DIMENSIONS
of TEAM

BOOKS BY
The Columbia Partnership Ministry Partners

George W. Bullard Jr.
Every Congregation Needs a Little Conflict
Pursuing the Full Kingdom Potential of Your Congregation

Richard L. Hamm
Recreating the Church:
Leadership for the Postmodern Age

Edward H. Hammett
Reaching People under 40 while Keeping People over 60:
Being Church to All Generations

Spiritual Leadership in a Secular Age:
Building Bridges Instead of Barriers

Making Shifts without Making Waves:
A Coach Approach to Soulful Leadership

A full listing and description of TCP resources are available at
www.chalicepress.com and
www.thecolumbiapartnership.org

SPIRITUAL DIMENSIONS
of TEAM

ALAN N. WRIGHT

CHALICE
PRESS

ST. LOUIS, MISSOURI

Cover art: FotoSearch

Cover and interior design: Elizabeth Wright

Visit Chalice Press on the World Wide Web at
www.chalicepress.com

10 9 8 7 6 5 4 3 2 1   10   11   12   13   14   15

EPUB: 978-08272-34796   EPDF: 978-08272-34802

Library of Congress Cataloging-in-Publication Data

Wright, Alan N.
Spiritual dimensions of team / Alan N. Wright.
p. cm.
Includes bibliographical references (p.   ).
ISBN 978-0-8272-3471-0
1. Group ministry. I. Title.
BV675.W75 2010
253—dc22   2009047116

Printed in United States of America

Contents

Editor's Foreword

Inspiration and Wisdom for Twenty-First–Century Christian Leaders

You have chosen wisely in deciding to study and learn from a book published in **The Columbia Partnership Leadership Series** with Chalice Press. We publish for

- Congregational leaders who desire to serve with greater faithfulness, effectiveness, and innovation.
- Christian ministers who seek to pursue and sustain excellence in ministry service.
- Members of congregations who desire to reach their full kingdom potential.
- Christian leaders who desire to use a coach approach in their ministry.
- Denominational and parachurch leaders who want to come alongside affiliated congregations in a servant leadership role.
- Consultants and coaches who desire to increase their learning concerning the congregations and Christian leaders they serve.

The Columbia Partnership Leadership Series is an inspiration- and wisdom-sharing vehicle of The Columbia Partnership, a community of Christian leaders who are seeking to transform the capacity of the North American church to pursue and sustain vital Christ-centered ministry. You can connect with us at www.TheColumbiaPartnership.org.

Primarily serving congregations, denominations, educational institutions, leadership development programs, and parachurch organizations, the Partnership also seeks to connect with individuals, businesses, and other organizations seeking a Christ-centered spiritual focus.

We welcome your comments on these books, and we welcome your suggestions for new subject areas and authors we ought to consider.

George W. Bullard Jr., Senior Editor
GBullard@TheColumbiaPartnership.org

The Columbia Partnership,
332 Valley Springs Road, Columbia, SC 29223-6934
Voice: 803.622.0923, www.TheColumbiaPartnership.org

Acknowledgments

I am grateful for all those experiences with teams, which have taught me so well—as a team member, leader, trainer, and coach. One of the great characteristics of those who work with groups and teams is open sharing of tips and tricks with colleagues. Most of what exists in your personal coach's toolbox of techniques or insights was handed down multiple times before you discovered it. Even when you seem to have created something new, upon reflection you can see the threads that tie it back to something else. The unfortunate part of this rich history in experiential learning is that it is hard to give credit to the originators because many times they remain anonymous. Every team I've been with has taught me something new—thank you.

Writing is a long process, and I would like to specifically thank several readers, coaches, or editors who helped me along the journey. Gloria Wright, Bruce McAllistar, and Elayne Vanasse all helped improve early versions. I would also like to thank George Bullard, the senior editor for The Columbia Partnership Leadership Series, for encouragement and support with the book proposal. California State University at Northridge should also be acknowledged, as the key project in my sabbatical semester was the completion of this manuscript. I also thank Pablo Jiménez and the staff at Chalice Press for bringing this book to completion.

Finally, my wife Shannon and our three youngest children—Megan, Tyler, and Kylie—are all due extra kudos for enduring the process of "the book" and the author's crazy antics while working at home. To the three oldest children already out of the house—Jessica, Joshua, and Benjamin—thanks for life lessons represented in the book.

Preface

The visionary hope for this book is to contribute to a movement that develops truly effective ministry teams in churches and parachurch organizations. Teams are a means to an end: that churches would become effective team-based organizations that will *do justice, show mercy, and invite all to walk humbly with their God* (Mic. 6:8, paraphrased).

The years of fun, rewards, and frustration I've experienced as a team coach and group facilitator are behind this book. These years have shown me both what makes teams work and the spiritual elements that ultimately cause teams to thrive or dive. Through a series of parables, models, and discussions, the book helps readers understand the complexity of teams, highlighting manageable "team principles" and the underlying "spiritual dimensions" that enable team performance.

"Team" has become such a buzzword that yet another book on teams may not seem necessary. But teams are essential for ministry organizations in today's world. To create a team-based church or parachurch organization requires training and coaching, not mere theory. What we do not need is another book merely extolling the values of "team." The unique contribution of this book is that it brings together in one message (1) a behavioral understanding of team effectiveness, (2) specific spiritual and biblical principles combined with those practices, and (3) powerful learning tools for coaches to move teams from theory to life practice. Creating spiritually healthy teams will have a tremendous impact on the church's mission in the world.

This book will help you in at least three ways. First, it will provide you a framework to develop a team-based organization by introducing a model that can be replicated with training. Second, the book will challenge you at a personal level to explore how to become a better team member and leader. The great teams are made from members who are spiritually healthy. Yes, the great team has good process and skills, but process alone is insufficient.

Effective teams are spiritually sound. Third, given that as a team coach and trainer I've become more and more concerned about how to bridge the gaps between knowing and doing, the book offers learning methods and coaching strategies to help individuals and teams close the gaps as they move from awareness to practice to integration.

Al Wright—December 2010

1

The Power of
Self-directed Teams

Michael Phelps became a media hero at the Beijing Olympics in his quest to be the first swimmer to win eight gold medals at a single Olympic games. However, only five of those eight medals were in individual events, while three came from team relay events. The 4 by 100 team relay event will stand out as a sports classic for years to come. Phelps, Garrett Weber-Gale, Cullen Jones, and Jason Lezak collectively set a new world record for the event. Each American swimmer was within fractions of a second ahead or behind their competitors in their respective legs. But, with the USA trailing France in the final leg, Jason Lezak swam the fastest 100-meter leg ever for a come-from-behind victory by 8/100ths of a second. The U.S. team beat the previous world record by four seconds. The team excelled and achieved a remarkable outcome. Every swimmer had turned in a world-class performance and, in the words of Jason Lezak, cited at the NBC Olympics Web site, "You know, this isn't a 4 by 100, this is a 400. We're a team."

Teams accomplish great things by the combined efforts of their members. Each member contributes, but in different ways. Centuries ago the apostle Paul created the best team metaphor to describe the work of the church—"the body of Christ" (1 Cor. 12:12–31). Different members of a team have different functions and that allows for the collective work to get done. "If they were all one part, where would the body be? As it is, there are many parts, but one body" (1 Cor. 12:19–20). Teams accomplish visions by the contributions of their members. What distinguishes a team from a group is a pragmatic principle—getting something done. Implement visions. Achieve results. Change the world.

The Western church today faces a tremendous challenge. The number of committed followers of Christ in the U.S. is in decline, as measured by regular church attendance.[1] Almost every mainline denomination is in decline.[2] American clergy are aging and the younger replacement leadership is not there.[3]

A reversal in this trend is possible if churches and parachurch ministries shift to team-based organizations. If the Western church continues with its current approach to ministry, then growth, outreach, and impact on culture will continue to diminish.

Traditional Church Organizations

The vast majority of churches are not organized as team-based organizations (TBO) with a visionary agenda. The common church organizational model is staff-driven rather than team-driven with an outreach orientation. The average church in America is small. Seventy percent have a worship attendance of 125 or less.[4] A church this size usually supports a professional staff (pastor) of one. Larger congregations add staff at a ratio of staff to membership of 1 to 59 according to an unpublished survey in 2006 by the Leadership Network. Pastors work extremely hard and the demand of providing "services" to the church membership is overwhelming. Clergy are working hard: giving of themselves, preaching, visiting the sick, and attending meetings. Today's pastors entering church ministry after seminary are leaving in increasing numbers due in part to the excessive demands and burnout.[5]

Pastors are not laboring completely alone. Volunteers are present at the core of church life. Small groups of volunteers give extraordinary amounts of time to the church's activities. While professional church staff still manage or supervise the bulk of church activities, and the additional management of these volunteers as part-time workers becomes a major time commitment for the full-time staff, these dedicated volunteers are vital to the success of congregations. No one has calculated the real numbers, but if "core volunteers" time was added up into full-time staff equivalents (40 hours per week), then the ratio of full-time staff to church attendees would rise. Still, the majority of attendees still remain on the edges as religious consumers, not passionately involved in the work of ministry.

Church organizations reflect the culture in which they live—less a generation or so. The church today represents an organizational pattern that came with the rise of modern industry. Though we think of churches as spiritual places with unique organizations, much of their look and function reflects the cultural context. I beg you to suspend traditional church language and theology for the moment and follow the parallel. Small business organizations (small churches) would have an owner (pastor) and a number of workers (church members). Larger business organizations (medium and larger churches) would have an executive leader (senior pastor) and multiple staff (managers) to supervise the key functional parts of the organization and its workers (church members).

Churches that operate with this traditional organizational pattern (with variable degrees of hierarchy and bureaucracy) will fall into one of two categories. Mission and vision will be *inward focused* or *outward focused*. Writers critical of the declining church point to the predominance of inward-focused versus outward-focuses churches.[6] The difference is critical from a missional perspective, but not from an organizational one. The organizational pattern is the same—staff-driven, linear, and hierarchical. A traditional inward-focused church will have pastors supervising how to meet the needs of the *current members* of the congregation. A traditional outward-focused church will simply have key pastors supervising volunteers to meet the needs of the *external community* who are not currently members.

The distinction between an outward-focused versus the inward-focused church *is* an important one from theological and missional perspectives. Theological arguments could be made on either side of the divide. In one sense, the dichotomy is a false choice, as a church should have both an inward and outward focus. But genuine balance is impossible. The church will tip one way or the other—usually a significant tilt. My clear bias is that the primary missional DNA should be outward focused (with an ongoing scramble to address inward issues). I raise this debate because it is important for reversing the current decline. However, I fear that even if magically all the churches became outward focused, the traditional organizational patterns would limit the impact.

The point of this chapter is to determine whether or not the church is a team-based organization. Change in how the church does ministry is imperative. My point is that team-based organizations offer a healthier, more effective way to accomplish the mission of the church.

The Team-based Organization (TBO)

What would happen if the church were a team-based organization (TBO) rather than a staff-supervisor style of organization? A TBO empowers teams to accomplish the mission rather than directing individual staff and volunteers to carry out that mission. There is a debate in organizational circles about who creates better vision and mission, the key leader or a visionary team. But let's avoid that debate and assume that the church embraces a compelling vision of a preferred future (whoever puts it together). The TBO creates a network of teams who are given the authority to accomplish all or parts of that compelling vision. TBOs have higher involvement, less turnover, faster implementation, and greater outcomes or results. TBOs also have less rigidity and more chaos, while gaining more creativity.

This is the bottom line for the church—teams have a multiplying effect. More people will accomplish more. Imagine if the team model replaced the traditional model of the church. Instead of an inner core of 10 percent of church members volunteering what they can do while pastors are doing *all* they can do, imagine 80 percent of church members volunteering what they can do. The role of the pastor changes tremendously in the TBO. The role of the volunteers (members) changes drastically as well. The missional results of the church are multiplied.

Teams bring more to churches and parachurch organizations than just productivity. Spiritually healthy teams also provide a secondary benefit of a vibrant sense of community. Effective teams create positive relationships, and people appreciate one another more. Teams also provide a key place for spiritual formation. The potential for significant growth in faith occurs in all organizational contexts. Spiritual issues are foundational to effective teams, so the potential for growth and discipleship is heightened.

Four Keys to Teams Working in Ministry Organizations
Key Leaders Need to Believe in Teams

The primary reason team-based organization fails in churches (or in business) is the lack of belief in teams. If the executive leadership (senior pastor or parachurch executive director) does not have a deep commitment to a team philosophy, the organization will not become a TBO. If the pastor is not fully committed to a team philosophy, teams won't work.

When I began working as a team consultant and coach, I would respond to any organization that wanted to do team development or team training programs. I no longer provide services just based on request. My new guideline is that assessment of executive leadership in the organization must occur before proceeding with team development strategies. There must be support for a TBO.

Leaders need to overcome the "everybody believes in teams" myth. Everybody wants the camaraderie and feel-good side of teams. Leaders and pastors want to have a team reputation. But team empowerment and a team-based organization is often not a core value. Many people believe they already have a teams philosophy in their organization. So what happens is that the consultant comes in, creates a great training program, staff get excited about new skills and new possibilities, and then executive leadership strips the team of genuine power and morale takes a nosedive. Middle managers or team leaders call the consultant and say: "I guess we weren't serious here about doing team." Meanwhile, executive leadership continues to live in the delusion that they support teams. Or executives develop a *been-there-done-that* belief and teams are relegated to a passing trend.

TBOs can have great variability in the format and structure of teams. Teams require certain values and the key leaders or the board need to see these values as central to who they are. Here are a few expressions of team values (not in order of priority).

- Power in the organization is shared (decentralized versus centralized).
- How things get done must enable teams to function (i.e., form must follow function—procedures, rules and regulations, etc.).
- Teams require effective leadership.
- A level of chaos is okay.
- Good function in teams is essential to avoid chaos.
- Spiritual development is central to teams.
- Creativity is good.
- Critical thinking is good.
- Results are important.
- Teaming requires training.

So let's assume for the moment that organizational assessment has taken place. The organization and its key leaders have a genuine commitment to embrace the values of a team organization. A commitment exists to empower teams to make key decisions and to implement their plans. Executive leadership will support and embrace these new ventures with the risk that some will be wildly successful and some will be significant failures. Bring on the training program. Let the teamwork begin.

Don't Confuse Team Development with Conflict Resolution

Key leaders must not confuse team training with conflict resolution. Organizations cannot expect team building and movement toward a TBO to resolve group conflict. Many believe that creating team building or team spirit will resolve interpersonal or organizational conflicts. Leadership mistakenly believes that a team program that makes people feel more connected will solve this unrelated organizational problem. That won't work. Conflicts in the church are probably anchored in issues that have little to do with organizational structure.

However, although TBOs are not the ultimate solution to conflicts, they can help an organization to work more effectively with conflict. Therefore, resolve the conflict issues first and then launch your program to transition to teams.

Overcoming the Attitude That Teams Don't Work

Churches can fail to develop team-based organizations because of a growing attitude that teams simply don't work. Many staff or volunteers in your organization will have been previously immersed in some kind of a team environment. At least, they went through something that was *labeled* a team. As the "team" buzzword has grown, more and more people have had a bad experience with a team process. Selling genuine teams is getting harder due to a negative stereotype in certain settings. Staff needs to be convinced that being team based will really make a positive difference.

One experience that gives teams a bad rap is the committee structure of many church organizations. Most committees are not teams. A committee can function as a very powerful team, but that is usually not the case. Some churches have renamed all their committees as teams, but then are surprised by the lack of results. What would be the difference between a traditional committee and a traditional team?

Committees classically manage predictable routine, whereas a team is focused on change. If the project is repetitive, such as an annual task within the organization, a team approach is focused on how that task can improve. Improved results are specific and clear. A team will keep the best of what has been done or perhaps reinvent the entire process. The results orientation is the key characteristic that separates teams from committees. Committees rarely measure results and cannot clearly define success or failure. Teams know their results.

Perhaps the most significant distinction between committee and team is how decisions are made. A team's results are tied to effective decision-making at meetings. Committees have a reputation for prolonged decision-making and endless meetings: "I can't believe how long last night's meeting went!" "Can you believe what people said at that meeting? I'm thinking of resigning from the committee." Effective teams do not have painful meetings. Death by committee (or ineffective team) is a terrible fate. Effective teams replace bad processes with healthy process.

Positive team meetings are an issue of both skill and spiritual maturity. Team meetings are discussed later on in chapters 7–8 and 13–14. Meetings can be stimulating and enjoyable. The real issue is convincing people that there is hope when we speak about team. As the old car ad says, "This isn't your father's [car]." Communicate that this is a new experience in team development and not a new name for that old committee process.

Team-based Organizations Require Training

Another reason churches fail to develop TBO is the presumption that training is not necessary. Ministry teams don't just happen any more than great music just happens. If you want a championship women's basketball team, the coach must do more than assemble five young women and throw them a basketball. Ministry teams or board teams need to develop skills and nurture their spiritual character so that effectiveness can flourish. Any good outcome stems in part from good training and design. Good intentions are not enough. Most volunteer organizations have a great example at their facility that symbolizes intention over competence. Not everyone can paint well, like a professional painter. Not everyone can install sheetrock like a professional tradesman. Teams need training to be effective. A TBO will have a program for training and maintaining teams.

Powerful Team Ministry

One of the best ministry experiences of my life was working with a highly effective team to train church leaders and impact their ministry organizations. That team experience reinforced an important insight about great teams: teamwork is about functionality. Hands and feet enable a body to move toward its goal. Skills in decision-making and creativity move a ministry team toward its goal. But functionality is tied to spirituality. Great teams are more about spiritual dimensions than functional dimensions. Failure to perform as a team is often due to issues of the human soul rather than a lack of skill and performance.

I sat with those ministry teammates reflecting and celebrating seven years of working together. The celebration setting was idyllic, looking out on the slopes of Mt. Hood from the comfort of the historic Timberline Lodge. The project team had been idyllic as well: working and laughing together, creating great friendships and great achievements. The conversation identified several important principles for team effectiveness.

The team had come together to develop an intervention and training program for a diverse set of parachurch organizations that shared a common vision to impact youth in their communities. The task was challenging, the initial funding meager, but positive results were unmistakable. As with all projects, there was a combination of some painful failures mixed with the rosy successes, but overall the project outcomes were decisively positive and measurable. The ministry organizations had gathered new visions, strengthened their boards, created innovative new programs, and raised their level of excellence. The team had made a difference for Christ and his kingdom.

Functional Dimensions of Team

How can teams make a difference? Team members can follow several key principles for teams. Part of this book describes those functional principles. Keeping four key team dimensions in rhythm creates positive team results. The functional dimensions are represented in the model below and include:

- *Share the power,* symbolized by balancing a stick
- *Achieve results,* symbolized by moving a rock
- *Tend to the emotional climate,* which is symbolized by a heart
- *Restore the energy and vitality,* symbolized by water

Effective Team Dimensions

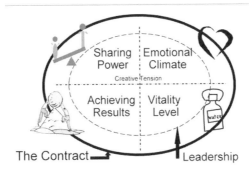

The four dimensions in the model can be evaluated and monitored separately. As with any complex model, overlap and significant interaction of the four dimensions exist. Leadership is defined primarily as an influence rather than a role in this model. This leadership influence directs the four key dimensions to sustain effectiveness. A team contract is the single most important tool a team has at its disposal. The contract is a key statement of the agreements that define who the team wants to be, becoming a tool to help the members achieve their vision. The use of the contract is more fully discussed in chapter 15. Creative tension stems from the team's problem-solving process. Tension is a good thing and contributes to great team results. Tension and its challenges are discussed in chapter 10.

Spiritual Dimensions of Team

Sharing power, moving the rock, monitoring climate, and managing vitality are all functions of leadership expressed by team members. Each dimension can be described at a behavioral or functional level. Skills related to those behaviors can be identified and practiced. But each functional area is tied to issues of the human spirit. Spiritual issues are foundational to the functional dimensions of teams, which frequently fail, not from a lack of skill or knowledge, but from spiritual immaturity. Team success is dependent on spiritual health. Team functionality is necessary but insufficient.

The project team described earlier had this self-reflection on the success of their team. The spiritual dimension of this team was unmistakably the key factor to the team's success. The superb problem-solving skills of the team were based on the members' years of experience in the field, but the most important key to success had been the "lack of egos in the room." This was a talented team with great skills, but everyone was able to let go of personal power needs and allow vision and ideas to rule the team rather than personal agenda. Without the ability to truly share power, a team never realizes its full potential. I do not want to minimize the importance of competence, but there is a *spiritual* competence that is even more foundational to team success.

This team had maintained a positive climate with one another through the years. High levels of respect and trust characterized its emotional climate. The team members showed fundamental care and concern for fellow team members. However, don't misunderstand and equate a positive climate with a lack of conflict. There was no absence of conflict and pressure. The care and support helped keep the tension positive rather than debilitating.

Beyond the results achieved, the sharing of power, and the positive climate, the team was known for its laughter and energy. Team meetings were not times of dread, but rather times of vitality. The team members had all been part of plenty of other work teams. What was it that made the difference? Playful banter was part of the fabric of the group and became both a symbol and a cause of the consistently high vitality level the team experienced at team meetings. Whether it was a multi-day planning retreat or a short conference call, the team remained engaged. Laughter at the serious and the mundane reflected people's total presence and ability to enjoy the moment. Play and refreshment became integrated into the hard work agenda. The ability to play well is a gift from God based in the theology of redemption and creation.

One way to look at the interrelated team dimensions is to imagine two pairs of glasses, each with a very different type of lens. One set of glasses is designed to reveal the functional dimensions of team. What are the fundamental team processes that must work well in order for the team to function at a high level? The high performance team becomes very skilled in using the functional lenses and is able to assess and intervene to maximize effectiveness. The second set of lenses looks at the same team and sees a different factor—much like night vision goggles that "see" infrared emission (heat) rather than visible light. Both lenses capture the same movement, but the assessment is different.

Individual team members contribute to the overall success of the team because of their spiritual health. In the subsequent chapters, the connection between the functional and spiritual dimensions will be unpacked. The spiritual beliefs team members hold and the consistency with which these beliefs are practiced is the background for all effective teamwork.

Disclaimers and Definitions

What Is a Team?

Most readers of this book already have some innate belief in teams. It is part of our cultural ethos that teamwork is a good thing. To be against team is like being against American icons such as motherhood, the Fourth of July, and baseball. But, what exactly is a team?

Team as used in this book is a *small group of people who share a common goal to achieve a specific result.* The team may be completely voluntary, such as a church outreach task force, or involuntary, such as an assigned task force at work. What differentiates a team from a group is that the team has a stake in a specific outcome or result. Groups may have no achievable external goal. Many groups are not teams, but *are* important groups—such as a Bible study group or a recovery group. Teams have a specific outcome that extends beyond creating community. The outcome may be a product or program, or perhaps gaining important new information, as in the case of a learning team.

The results orientation is the key factor that separates a team from a group, but there are other key pieces that make up a team as well. Teams have *real time interactions* between members (as do groups). I was once a member of a team that never met. The organization had labeled us a team, but we were not a team, and of course there was no tangible outcome. Team meetings can be virtual or face-to-face. Teams have a beginning and an end; this cycle of life is an important part of the team process.

A team must have some level of *self-determination.* There are a variety of teams in the lives of organizations: vision teams, functional teams, cross-functional teams, design teams, and executive teams. Almost all of them could be grouped into three categories: (1) pseudo (or fake) teams, (2) implementation or functional teams (aligned along functions in the organization), and (3) vision teams. The distinction is based on the scope or level of self-determination. Vision teams set overall direction for the organization. The self-determination is extensive because of the overarching role of vision in organizations. Functional teams work with the traditional operational areas in the organization. A parachurch organization might have a marketing team, a fund development team, or a program team. In a local church the functional teams might be organized around traditional ministries, such as youth, hospital care, or outreach. The most important team to describe at this juncture is the pseudo team.

The *fake team* lacks self-determination. Just because you call something a dog does not make it a dog. If it walks like a dog, looks like a dog, and smells everything in its world, then we've got ourselves a dog. As "team" became more of a buzzword in the last two decades, there have been an extraordinary number of mistaken identifications. A team must have at least three characteristics: an identifiable outcome, a group of people who interact to produce that result, and the power to create the desired result.

Many so-called teams in organizations are pseudo teams because they do not control their destiny. Executive teams in ministry organization are rarely teams because the organization's power structure is too hierarchical. Many churches *name* teams, but the power to implement plans is so compromised by the trustee board or elder board that team cannot really happen. Organizational cultures that value centralized control and autocratic leadership will end up with a number of fake teams. Money is a great marker for decision-making authority, and, if money is not distributed within the organization, then the power is usually not distributed and real teams won't be present.

Self-directed Teams

True teams can be organized along a leadership continuum identifying who holds responsibility for team process and effectiveness. A true team always shares responsibility for attaining final results. The leadership role directing the team process can belong to several different entities. A self-directed team names everyone responsible for effective team process as well as outcomes—meaning the members of the team share that leadership responsibility. Teams can shift the responsibility for process to a specific role, such as an internal team leader or external team coach. A specific team leader role may come from a team vote or it might be a role assigned by the organization.

This book has a strong bias for the self-directed team who can learn the team functions and develop the strategies to monitor their team function. This shared leadership function replaces an internal leadership role or an external team coach or consultant. As the team members learn the process and some of the tools, the self-directed team becomes a reality. The self-directed team has three great advantages. First, ownership of process as well as results helps motivate the team. Second, the cost savings across a church organization is significant as the need for external coaching expertise is reduced. Third, a learned culture of doing team eventually permeates the organization so that the team-based ministry organization truly exists.

2

How to Create Spiritually Transformed Teams

The Question of Transformation

Building effective leadership and teams is about transformation. How do we really make things happen? Making changes is the real challenge. What changes need to be made in a team to create effectiveness? If spiritual dimensions are foundational to teamwork, how does spiritual transformation occur?

Exploring spiritual dimensions of team pushes to the center one of the greatest questions about the human condition. How do you bring about spiritual transformation or spiritual formation? Theologians, religious educators, psychologists, and organizational change specialists have asked the question. Cynics and determinists would claim that change is not possible. Optimists advocate for change, but do not necessarily know how to create it. The hope for this book is to address the strategies that can create change in team members and the team itself by exploring how we create personal spiritual change. To answer this challenge, certain assumptions need to be identified.

Spirituality

One approach to spirituality is to relegate it to a box of a certain shape and size. This compartmentalization is quite popular in faith communities in particular, and Western culture in general. Church people often relegate spiritual practice to certain rituals that occur in a specific time and place. These rituals might be individual, such as prayer and reading the Bible, or might be community based as the group gathers for worship and study on a regular schedule. A spiritual model such as this puts a circle around spiritual things and a separate circle around secular things.

Another approach to spirituality is to see it integrated into every aspect of life, where there is no separation between one moment or activity and the next. An integrated approach connects belief and life experiences throughout each day of the week and throughout a total lifestyle—from home to work to leisure to church.

Spirituality at its core focuses on the inner world of what we truly believe and what we desire—the matters of the heart. An integrated approach to spirituality combines this inner world of beliefs and motivations with the outer world of behavior and practices. Genuine spirituality is integrated.

Spiritual Transformation—*Gapology*

The second assumption about making spiritual (or functional) changes is that transformation focuses on the gaps that exist between the *ideal* and the *real*. I believe that most people have a desire or hope to be spiritually healthy or alive. Most people want to be kinder, gentler, more gracious, and wiser. Desire alone is inadequate to produce lasting change, and everyone falls short of the mark (Rom 3:23). For some, life has been so dark and twisted that even this base desire has been eliminated and evil has become monstrous—but that is a discussion for another time. For most followers of God, God's new work is to strengthen the hope and desire for new life and healing (holiness, righteousness). The challenge for those of us on that journey is overcoming our gaps between our desired future and the current reality of our day-to-day life (brokenness). The illustration below identifies the three types of gaps that keep us from God's transformation of our lives.

Gapology is the author's term for the study of the gaps between the current reality of a team or person and the desired new reality. Three kinds of gaps challenge individuals and teams. A Type I Gap is between knowing in general and knowing at the personal level—personal awareness. Leaders today are great at knowing the importance of good communication and may think they have great communication skills, when in fact their staff would tell a different story. The self-awareness gap exists not only for skills but for

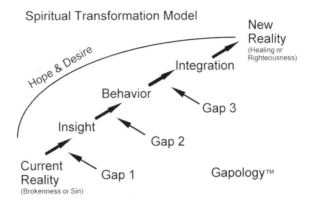

Spiritual Transformation Model

spiritual issues as well. The gap in spiritual self-awareness is far harder to identify than a skill but is equally important.

The greatest challenge of Gapology is the gap between *new insight* and *behavior*, or, more aptly, behavioral consistency (Type II Gap). Let's assume a person knows he is egocentric in his motivation toward team involvement and wants to be more other-conscious in attitude and behavior. Gap I is closing from this self-awareness. Chances are that the actions that demonstrate other-conscious attitude are occasional. This second gap represents a clear intention to act but a failure to behave as we desire on a consistent basis. Closing the gap between that intention and day-to-day behavior is a great challenge. But change is possible. It may seem as though the self-centric person is doomed forever; however, with a readiness for change there can be movement in the team-centered direction. A Gap II is closed when new behaviors become consistent.

The third gap is internal, between our *behavior* and our *intention*. This may sound like the second gap, but the distinction here is deeply spiritual. When the Gap II is obvious in someone else, we label it hypocrisy. I am trying and I know I am falling short of the goal. There is a type of hypocrisy where my walk does not match my talk, but I am clear in acknowledging that gap. There is another kind of hypocrisy where my walk appears fairly consistent but there is no match between my behavior and my inner motives. For example, I might extend to you words of kindness or encouragement at a behavioral level, but my inner world feels no sense of care or concern for you. In other words, there is no consistency or congruence between my observable behavior and my inner motivation.

The congruence gap creates persons who lose their souls, believing to be one thing when in fact they are something else. Discussion follows later on the methods that keep us on a path of integration and congruence versus a path of incongruence and disintegration.

Spiritual Development Methods

Assume that a person is willing to recognize the gaps that exist in her spiritual development. How do you close the gaps? There is not a simplistic step-by-step process to move from low-life to sainthood. But pastors, teachers, and spiritual directors over the years have identified some methods and approaches that can help move us along. Gap closing methods will be highlighted throughout the book, and the roles of trainer and coach are introduced. The figure below shows spiritual transformation methods. Spiritual competence can be impacted through coaching, the power of group (POG), story and metaphor, habits of virtue, personal reflection, life challenges, and mystical transformation. The terms are identified in the diagram below, and later chapters will discuss a spiritual formation method as a tool for impacting team member spirituality.

A Coach Approach to Spiritual Formation

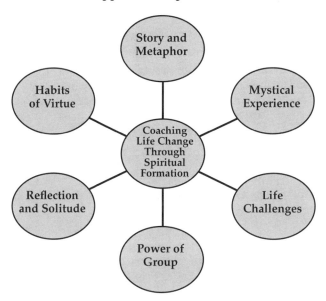

Coaching as the Meta-Method for
Spiritual Team Development

Coaching is a method of closing gaps using a toolbox full of methods and skills. *Coaching* is a word like *team*; everybody uses it and everybody means something different. In this book, a coach is a multi-contextual "gapologist." A coach is someone who helps the person being coached to close a gap. The gap may be a spiritual gap, or any other kind of gap between a desired end and the person's current reality. The Person Being Coached (PBC) or Team Being Coached (TBC) defines the gap and the coach becomes a thinking partner to help the PBC or TBC build the new bridge over the gap. The coach applies her skills in a variety of different contexts.

The role of the coach in creating powerful teams is to assist team members individually and the team as a unit. The coach can address functional dimensions of team as well as spiritual dimensions. Coaching for spiritual change is viewed as a meta-method because the coaching process introduces other classic methods for spiritual transformation. For an outstanding introduction to Christian coaching, read Jane Creswell's book *Christ-Centered Coaching*.[1] Let's describe briefly the coach approach for those not familiar with this method.

Effective coaching is based on a number of important principles: some better understood as skills and some best defined as attitudes or values. The PBC or TBC chooses a coach to explore an important issue. The coach intentionally takes on the duty to walk with the person being coached toward new discoveries and new actions. The PBC enters the coaching relationship with an expectation of taking action around the PBC's gaps. "No action, no coaching," is an oft-heard mantra in coaching circles and is a key characteristic that separates coaching from other types of helping methods. The coach guides action planning, but the actions chosen are the domain of the PBC.

The coaching conversation is the structure of the coaching process, and the coach brings a number of skills to that conversation. This conversation may be with an individual or with the entire team. The coach is able to listen at multiple levels, hearing accurately what is expressed by the TBC. As the coach listens to the issue presented, a manageable topic becomes the focal point. A question that helps focus and clarify is: What do you want? More specifically, what is the hope, the outcome, the change that you would like to see? Through the use of powerful questions, the issue is narrowed down, much like the dividing point between the upper and lower sections of an hourglass.

As the conversation continues, the coach encourages the person or team to focus on options to achieve. Pursuit of these options might involve broadening the creative thinking process, or it might involve challenging a limiting belief or crashing through an apparently insurmountable roadblock. The coaching process explores potential action and its consequences, resulting in a specific set of steps that the team can identify as a path of action.

Coaching becomes more than just guiding a TBC through an analytical sequence of problem-solving steps, although it certainly embraces that tradition. A great coach holds up a mirror and challenges the assumptions and thoughts of the team being coached. The coach challenges, but she also motivates with the words of encouragement. The coach creates an emotional synergy that proclaims a belief in other persons, even when they may not have the power of that belief in themselves.

Coaching can also be described by what it is *not*. Coaching is not a process of telling. Spiritual coaching especially is not about moral telling or parenting advice about what a person should do. The person being coached is the agent of discovery, and in spiritual coaching the PBC interacts with the Holy Spirit as the process unfolds. A coach is not a mentor. A mentor is primarily a teller who shares from what he has found helpful on a similar path he traveled at an earlier time. Nor does a coach serve as a consultant. A consultant is traditionally another type of teller based on development of a current area of expertise. A team consultant would evaluate and tell a team about a dysfunction. A team coach would guide the team through a process of self-discovery about the dysfunction and how to make things different. This does not mean a coach will not share resource and expertise, but it is not a primary focus. Finally, a coach is not a passive listener who only responds and gently guides the person along a sequential process. Great coaches do so much more that is active and full of passion and courage for their clients.

Spiritual Tools for the Coach

Great coaches understand the challenges of change both for individuals and for teams. The coach will disclose a number of development strategies to help people move successfully over their gaps. The spiritual coach is a gapologist who understands the following methods for spiritual change.

- The power of *reflection* involves strategies such as reflective conversation, journaling, and solitude, all with the purpose of personal discovery about the person being coached and her spiritual journey. Reflection involves more than introspection because it invites other objective information into the reflection cycle, such as team member feedback or videotape playback. Reflection also invites the Holy Spirit into the center of the reflective process.
- The *POG or power of the group* is transformative as it goes beyond providing feedback to harnessing the power of encouragement from others and the power found in group accountability.
- *Stories and metaphors* are great guides along the path of spiritual development. Everyone remembers and retells powerful stories. Stories and metaphors are influential tools for change.
- Effective *habits* are the no-brainer method for developing consistency and quality in musicians, surgeons, and athletes. Teams and their members benefit from developing good habits in their functional process. Development of *habits of virtue* becomes critical for spiritual formation.
- *Life challenge* is the most loved and hated friend one can have. In the crucible of tough times the most significant growth and change can occur. No one remembers the ship's voyage in which everything went smoothly and the waters were quiet and serene, but everyone remembers the storming sea, the torn sail, and the vanishing sun against a rocky coastline. The desperate search for that harbor and place of shelter is memorable and produces change. The greatest development in the maturity of our souls is found in meaningful challenge.
- *Mystical experiences* are a special category of spiritual formation and will be briefly discussed. The direct work of grace in our lives through the Holy Spirit will always remain a mystery. Readiness for those experiences is part of the process. Trails off the main road can create the most interesting surprises on the journey.

3

Sharing Power in Teams

The Parable of the Big-Stick Family

Once upon a time an old beaver ruled a beaver colony. The colony had been around forever and now faced starvation. As the colony grew over time, it had devastated the food supply near the dam. The colony was so large now that a second colony had formed, and now both were starving. Something had to be done, and each colony's decisions were made in very different ways.

The original colony family we'll call the Big-Stick Family because the colony was ruled by a single leader with a strong voice and a powerful big stick. A colony meeting was called about the food crisis. The leader was a very talented strategist and problem solver. As the meeting began, the *go-further-inland-for-food* plan was announced. "Live where we are and drag food back to the beaver pond." No one spoke up or questioned the plan, because the head beaver made all the decisions and the younger beavers quivered for fear of the big stick's punishing blow. "Execution follows planning—trust me on this." The old beaver had pairs organized and searching for food immediately. "Get busy! We need food now and for winter. Get to work!" he bellowed. The six other beavers in the colony jumped into their assigned actions to avoid the Big-Stick Beaver.

Meanwhile, the new colony called itself the Lever-Beaver Family because they expressed leadership in a very different way. In fact, there were many leaders who balanced leadership like a lever on a fulcrum. A favorite Lever-Beaver Family game was using a log over a log like a teeter-totter on a children's playground. The teeter-totter game represented how the shared leadership model worked in their family team; one beaver up in the air as a leader and then the other beaver up in the air to lead.

The Lever team knew the serious problem before them, and called a family meeting to create a solution. A lively discussion ensued, full of enthusiasm and new ideas. The many voices bordered on chaos until one beaver tossed a stick into the middle of the circle, "Only one at a time, please!" Folks took turns, pushing the stick around like a dial on an old clock to point to the speaker. Pros and cons were voiced, and then a decisive plan all in quick time. Sharing power created enthusiastic support for the plan. The plan was ready to launch. Symbolically, the launch was like a new use of levers. Imagine the *new plan* on one end of the board, a fulcrum in the middle, and six excited beavers ready to jump on the opposite end. Exploration was the plan. Divide into pairs and explore the area: one pair downstream, a pair upstream on the left fork, and a third pair on the right fork. The fun-loving beavers devised a lever to catapult the explorers up into air, splashing down into the water, swimming away on their journeys. The search was on for new territory providing good food and good lodging.

The Levers met again in two days. Reports were made, opportunities discussed, and a decision finalized to head upstream. An old abandoned beaver lodge and dam was discovered, now lush with new vegetation. Everyone was excited at the great outcome: new home, new pond, immediate food, and easy work to gather more food for the upcoming winter.

As the Lever-Beaver colony prepared to leave for "greener pastures" the Big-Stick Family reported terrible news. The *go-further-inland-plan* had had dangerous consequences over the last two days. A wolf captured one beaver, with his coworker barely escaping to share the story. One beaver was crushed by a big tree falling the wrong way, as the beaver's fear of predators had encouraged an attempt at cutting big trees near the dam rather than little saplings farther away. Shaken by the tragedies, but still following the traditional leader, the old colony would lose two more to starvation during the upcoming winter.

Important differences differentiate the Big-Stick Family and the Lever-Beaver Family. Listen to the teamwork secrets in the symbol of sticks.

The Parable Interpretation

Sharing the power of decision is the fundamental principle of a high performance team. Ministry organizations pursue goals with different types of leaders and work teams. In the case of the Big-Stick Beaver, a leader is empowered for decision and he marshals groups to carry out his plan. Authority is held by one, or a select few, and the big stick of power enforces compliance, but motivation diminishes over time. A strong leader can be very skilled and create good plans. But plans without input from others can fail miserably if the single leader does not foresee the consequences. The best thinking in the group may never be heard when only one voice matters. The single beaver's big stick is a symbol of centralized power used to motivate others through fear and punishment.

An alternate model of getting things done shares the strategic decisions among team members. Leadership is still strong and decisive, but emerges in a different way. Members share power through many voices and tap the full human resources available. The Lever-Beaver Family used sticks to balance power by creating efficient ways to share many voices. Leadership is something dynamic that can move throughout the members of a team. Great ideas are shared and best plans are designed. Empowered teams create enthusiastic support that is essential to leverage highly successful outcomes.

Sharing power demands a commitment to an inclusive process. Poorly managed process enslaves teams to painful meetings followed by low achievement, but well-balanced *process* makes meetings fun and gets the work done. The Lever family was able to meet, create, analyze, act, and have fun in a way that surpassed the contribution of any single member on their team and led to a successful outcome.

Sticks can be used to build dials, levers, and fulcrums and create a picture of balancing power by sharing voice and leadership, maximizing strengths in the team, and reaching visionary plans.

Four key principles of effectiveness create successful self-directed teams; the first key is *sharing power* (symbolized by balancing a stick).

Leadership in teams involves influencing the four key processes toward sustained effectiveness. A contract is the key statement of values that define who the team can become, and a simple and powerful tool to regulate the team's character and performance.

Effective Team Dimensions

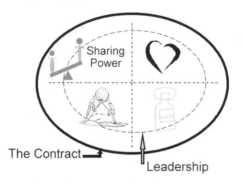

Sharing Power as a Functional Dimension of Team

Sharing power is one of the four key functional dimensions of team. The graphic represents these dimensions and their corresponding symbols. A stick creates a simple and effective mechanical lever. Sharing power defines the existence of a team and increases effectiveness much like a lever increases mechanical advantage.

The need for power is normal and healthy. Psychologist Dr. William Glasser in his book *Choice Theory*[1] argues through his theory of human behavior that each person has a need to exercise power. Power is our ability to influence the events around us. Exercise of power is a good thing. Power in teams is represented by the ability to have input and impact on team decisions.

Voice is the key indicator of power dynamics in a team. In all relationships we feel empowered when heard or valued by others. In the car ride to school one day, my son insisted on a position of power. Pushed out of conversation by his older and younger sisters, he shouted, "Please don't interrupt me; I've got something to say." That statement cuts to the heart of team member power—the need to be heard. Teams need to share the airtime to hear multiple voices.

Sharing airtime does not require each team member extracting equal minutes for individual use. A quieter person can enter a key comment and achieve adequate power. The important principle is that team members believe they are heard when they speak.

The Leadership Factor of Sharing Power

Voice in the team is the key indicator of sharing power, but the power dimension goes beyond voice alone. Power is expressed in decisions. Leadership is a decision-making process. The level of influence in decisions is a measure of power. How does leadership function best in teams? Is leadership a role or an influence? Can effective decisions be made by a full team, or should decisions be left to someone in a specific leadership role? Should a team have input while still leaving the ultimate decision-making responsibility in the hands of one leader?

Leadership is best understood as an influence in the overall process of the team rather than as a specific role given to a person. Leadership can be a role, but it must be viewed dynamically. Leadership in teams is shared. Team leadership is like the wind passing through the trees: seen by everyone but not easily tied to a single source.

The danger in shared leadership is the chaos of many voices. Decentralizing the power throughout the team can lead to long meetings and agonizing process. Is the benefit of input and motivation worth the time cost? The inefficiency concern can be avoided by maintaining two key principles—one procedural and one spiritual.

The procedural principle is a leadership skill. Meetings don't need to be a near-death experience. Procedures for managing input and building consensus and meeting deadlines can be developed by the self-directed team. The skill of keeping things moving will be described later in chapters 6 and 8. A team sharing power through dynamic leadership influence can maintain high efficiency. The link between a solitary leadership role and higher efficiency is debatable.

The spiritual principle of shared leadership influence provides efficiency and effective process. The old adage, "There is no *I* in *team*," is misguided. There are plenty of *I*'s in team because personal opinions and ideas are the creative heart of team. The spiritual principle is a willingness to set aside our personal power represented in ideas and statements. The ability to defer to others or to a larger goal is the spiritual foundation of teams.

Spiritually mature people are committed to a greater good and are quite willing to let go of personal ideas when a colleague's idea is even more powerful. High commitment to vision creates readiness to defer to others. No need for hours of discussion to get to a decision. Consensus is not about getting *my way* but on getting the best decision. Teams can move quickly when deference is the law of the team.

Is there a place for a team that is vision-centered, shares leadership, and still has a specific *team leader*? What role does the CEO play in an executive leadership team of a parachurch organization? What role does the senior pastor play in a group of ministry team leaders? Some teams are best designed with an equal distribution of power. Other teams design a differential level of power in leadership roles. The use of playing cards can help describe this not-totally-equal design.

When playing games of strategy, such as *Hearts,* certain cards are given a special power—trump cards. The CEO role in a ministry organization needs to identify what trump cards she holds. The right to hire or fire might be a CEO trump card. Other teams hire and fire by team decision. What key powers are given to the team and what powers are tied to a specific leadership role are variable. Trump cards are identifiable both in cards and teams and are kept to an important minimum.

Here are some possible trump cards: to monitor alignment with mission as defined by the board; immediate decisions; to be a tie-breaker when consensus does not exist. Define what cards will be held and keep them limited. If the leader holds too many trump cards, there is no *minimum empowerment factor* and therefore no team. If the pastor trumps any strategy created by the ministry team it will destroy the team. A mature leader backs off on his special project idea when the team has found a better strategy. Keep an ace, a king, perhaps a royal flush, depending on the team. There is no game when all the tricks are predictable. The *minimum factor of shared power* varies from team to team. The organizational opportunity is to increase the level of empowerment. As empowerment increases so will motivation, creativity, and accountability.

Perception is the secret of shared power. Spiritually healthy teams define expectations and limits of power at an early stage of their development. The rubber meets the road when an established team evaluates their current perceptions of power sharing. The coach's *Power Tools Toolbox* (chapter 5) shares some specific strategies to assist teams to evaluate their power sharing.

The Process Factor of Sharing Power

Fear can immobilize people. A bad experience creates fear of similar future experiences. Fear of empowered teams floundering about is a realistic concern. But full team empowerment and high team effectiveness can come together when both spiritual health and good team methodology are present.

What if a self-directed team could enjoy the benefits of empowerment without falling prey to the dangers of dysfunctional meetings? A few simple principles can keep power sharing efficient.

Team Consensus Model—Must We Agree?

"In essentials, unity; in nonessentials, diversity; in all things, charity." This saying, which origin is disputed, works well for teams. Reject the notion that team empowerment means total consensus for decisions. Sharing power does not mean 100 percent agreement on every issue. A personal belief model is a good metaphor to explain how group consensus should work. Picture your values and beliefs as three concentric circles. The inner circle represents *core beliefs*—those things that could not be compromised without a loss of integrity and identity. Belief strength increases as we move to our core. The core is smaller than the outer circles. Too large of a core creates difficult people because they bring the strength of core beliefs to their entire view of the world. Fundamentalism (religious or political or tactical) has a larger core than more flexible world views.

A second circle would be described as important beliefs. Important beliefs are just that—important but not critical. The outer circle or third circle is that world of information and belief that is nonessential. The same belief—Sabbaths are for resting—could be a core belief for some and "third-circle" belief for others. The point is that our reality is organized this way. Small inner circles generally represent more flexible people. Now, if the circle is too small, the person may lack substance. The "important beliefs" circle must also be appropriate in size or compromise is difficult.

Each person chooses how to balance the deference to other's beliefs against a commitment to personal core truth. *Balance* is appropriate self-denial held in tension with an uncompromised commitment to core beliefs. How this tension is defined speaks clearly to how one will engage fellow team members.

Teams should view issues and decisions in the same way as we have just described beliefs. Critically important issues ask for higher energy to achieve consensus. Less important issues can be delegated to the diversity of individual members in the team. On important issues, such as strategy direction or key policies, use a consensus style model. However, don't waste the team's time on detail issues.

The Five Levels of Agreement

This model combines the personal belief model with reaching decisions with other team members. Rather than three circles of personal belief, envision five *levels of consensus* that are based on levels of agreement in teams. Life is easy when a team is at Level 5 on a big issue. Life is hard when a big issue is stuck at Level 1. The goal of every team is to live and work in the lower levels whenever possible. Decisions and issues can avoid Level 1 the majority of the time.

The Five Levels of Agreement in Teams

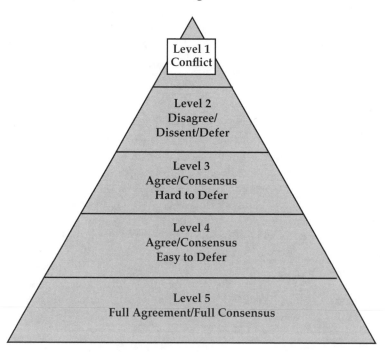

Level 1
Conflict

Level 2
Disagree/
Dissent/Defer

Level 3
Agree/Consensus
Hard to Defer

Level 4
Agree/Consensus
Easy to Defer

Level 5
Full Agreement/Full Consensus

Each level is described from the perspective of a team member's behaviors and final position of agreement with the team decision.

- Level 5: I listen; I understand; I agree; and I stand with you in agreement. Classic consensus is reached with various levels of enthusiasm but full agreement can exist. Full consensus by the team is celebrated and team life is easy.

- Level 4: I stand with you for unity. Consensus is embraced not because of shared value in the decision but because there is no conflict between personal beliefs and the team decision. Personally it's nonessential. Deferment is easy.

- Level 3: I listen; I understand; I disagree; it *is important*. However, I stand with you for unity. The team achieves full consensus because team members are willing to defer to others. The commitment to sharing power (cooperation) is based on the spiritual concept that I do not always get my way—even on important issues. I can embrace the team decision. Spiritually immature team members begin to stumble badly at this level.

- Level 2: I listen; I understand; I disagree; it *is important. I respect your view, but I must stand alone*. If I listen well, understand diversity, and do not assume that my conclusions are always right, I find a way to respect your viewpoint. When a level of difference is significant enough, I want to clearly identify myself as a dissenter to the team view. Spiritually healthy people do not need to block decisions at Level 2. Integrity pushes the person to voice concerns. A team's respect for that difference allows the dissenters to feel heard and understood. The dissenters can still respect and find value in the majority view so agreement can proceed.

- Level 1: I listen; I understand; I disagree; and it *is critically important. I cannot respect your view, but I still value you and I must stand alone*. Level 1 is the potential block to team decision because in this case the opposing argument or option is not valued. Differences in analysis or opposing core beliefs lead to a deeper level of disagreement. At this point continue to make the effort to separate the people from the issue. I may strongly disagree with my team member's strategy, but I need not disrespect the other team member as a person.

The test of a team's emotional and spiritual health is whether the primary emotion is profound sadness or anger at the final decision in Level 1. Sadness is tied to a sense of failure to persuade on something that really matters. Recognition that a key opposing value exists brings an inherent sense of separation, which evokes sadness. However, feelings of not being heard or feeling undervalued by the team can evoke anger. Separation of issues from persons, coupled with high levels of listening and understanding, will enable disagreements themselves to be processed in a manner that will not debilitate the team.

Teams must worry about consensus only on essentials. Does a profound disagreement (Level 1) mean the end of team? Absolutely not! Keep things in perspective. One decision among many does not destroy my attachment to the team.

Can a team decision be so important and disagreement so high that team loyalty and membership is at stake? Sure. A watershed decision may require departure from the team. Shallow people fabricate watershed issues when the real issue is unwillingness to defer on important beliefs. A true watershed assessment has genuine conflict at the core belief levels and departure might make perfect sense and can be done with honor, respect, and a dose of humility for all involved. Why humility? Only the future will determine who is more or less correct, and nobody controls the future.

The full range of options in the consensus model creates a level of freedom for team members. Focus team decisions on essentials. Leave the details to individuals. View consensus as a full range of options not as a restrictive, narrow process. Empower the team through spiritual development and good process that brings efficient decision-making. The toolbox in chapters 5 and 8 provides resources for quicker decisions that honor sharing power.

4

Spiritual Issues of Shared Power in Teams

Teams do not work very well when team members do not know how teams should work. If knowledge alone is the answer, then the multitude of training and development programs available to organizations should have fixed all teams by now. Knowledge and skills about team principles are important, but the biggest issues are spiritual.

Think about a time you observed a team not working together. Was there a major disagreement within the team? What would it have taken to get agreement and to have the team work together? Had the team lost its way? What would it have taken for each team member to pull in the same direction toward successful results? The tough issues of team are tied to questions of spiritual transformation. How willing are you to make personal changes to become part of a great team?

Personal Flexibility

Are you flexible enough to be a good team player? The human body has great flexibility. Flexibility is one of the classic dimensions of total fitness, along with cardiovascular fitness, strength, and agility. When was the last time you could bend over and touch your toes with your fingers? A child has a natural degree of flexibility that disappears later. Flexibility in bodies can be measured and it can be changed. Flexibility in your spirit or attitude can change too.

A willingness to bend frames the spiritual issue of sharing power. Openness to others' ideas models flexibility. Students or children are often described as *teachable* or *unteachable* by adults. Teachable indicates openness to hear new information. The unteachable child (or adult) is unwilling to recognize the teacher as a source of new information.

When Jesus came to earth, the religious leadership was inflexible. Jesus was expected to hang out with the "holy people" and was criticized for hanging out with the "party crowd." As Jesus noted:

> To what can I compare this generation? They are like children sitting in the marketplaces and calling out to others:
>
> > "We played the flute for you,
> >   and you did not dance;
> > we sang a dirge,
> >   and you did not mourn."
> > (Mt. 11:16–17).

Christ and John the Baptist both failed to meet the expectations of the religious establishment. Inflexibility keeps us from hearing and seeing new possibilities. Team members who are locked into a rigid, fixed picture of what should happen are not flexible. Sharing personal power in teams is not possible without flexibility.

If flexibility is the goal, the question becomes: What keeps us in the rigidity of inflexibility? The hard-wiring issue in humans for a *need for order* and differences in temperament are not the issue. The issue is controlling the world around us in order to achieve our self-centered ambitions. "Self-centered" is a tough term I'd rather ignore. But "self-centered" begins at our core in a natural or healthy sort of way. When my body gets thirsty I want a drink. When a friend makes me laugh I want to enjoy that person's company again. The problem with self-centeredness is the strength of the signal. The self focus needs to be tempered with a strong focus on others.

The challenge is how to move from an egocentric view of self to one that honors others above us. "Do nothing out of selfish ambition or vain conceit, but in humility consider others better than yourselves. Each of you should look not only to your own interests, but also to the interests of others" (Phil. 2:3–4). To put others' ideas above your own is to look to their interests and to treat them as people of equal or greater value. To put your ideas ahead of mine works against my selfish ambition. Every time I flex and give, I can become more flexible and increase my ability to share power.

One of the ways to test for flexibility is to measure our reactions to those around us. Do you critique first or affirm first when someone suggests a new idea? Western culture is steeped in critical analysis, and a natural pattern emerges to first see the flaws in an idea before looking at the strengths. Edward DeBono's problem-solving system speaks of this as the "Black Hat thinking skill."[1] Black Hat thinking is essential and important, but it should not be our leading response—especially in creative problem solving.

An idea is separate from the person. Healthy people differentiate their ideas from themselves. Yet people show natural attachment to their ideas. After all, they are *my* ideas. Initial criticism of ideas can make the person feel diminished. To see value first rather than criticism honors a person. Listen first, affirm second, and analyze third. A practical test of this principle is to make a list today of each time you hear a new suggestion—from where to go to lunch to a new idea at work. Think first of how to honor each idea rather than immediately evaluate it and criticize it.

A second flexibility test involves asking how you respond when hearing criticism directed toward you or your ideas. Is defensiveness and blame the first response, or is accepting responsibility the response? Defensiveness is a natural behavioral mechanism for self-protection, but defensiveness is over the top when it is consistently our first and primary reaction.

Teachers remember the student who always has an "excuse" for the unfinished homework. Excuses can be endless: the assignment was given too late, it got left at home, the computer went down. Do we have a routine of excuses? The next time someone asks a question about your current project, ask: Do I seek to blame or do I seek to accept responsibility? Admitting you've come up short demonstrates openness, flexibility, and emotional health. The more fragile the sense of self, the more vigorously we defend it. The more robust the self, the easier it is to accept appropriate responsibility.

A third simple behavior to test for a flexible spirit is to ask yourself if you interrupt others and finish their sentences. In some cultural contexts this behavior is more acceptable than in others. My impatience to listen sends the message: *my words are more important than your words.* If my words are viewed as more important, then I have put myself in the category of excessive self-importance and am less willing to honor you. Flexibility increases as we value others more. Rigidity increases as we become more self-absorbed.

Letting Go of Personal Privilege

People of privilege are less cooperative or flexible. I flew occasionally for years and then for several years became a road warrior that flew every week. Airlines give frequent flyers special privileges, such as early boarding or first class seating upgrades. Once a privilege is given, a new expectation is created. People of privilege expect special service.

A culture-of-comfort is provided to almost everyone in the West compared to global standards. The minimums of comfort have all been redefined. Take something simple such as hot water. If an American is denied hot water for a shower, frustrated calls are made to the spouse, water company, plumber, or whoever is deemed responsible for the lack of hot water. Hot water is a privilege that is not necessary for life. People in much of the world survive fine without it. Hot water is a great thing, but it bestows privilege. Privilege changes our attitude. Technological improvements redefine privilege almost monthly. People are regularly frustrated today with a cell coverage limitation or an older computer that is (compared to a new one) painfully slow.

As comfort has increased, people grow more privileged and expect life to cater to them. The list is long, but the expectation for a privileged life in every arena is on the rise. Follow the chain: increased comfort leads to increased expectation, an increased perception of control, and a distorted sense of power based on entitlement. To say it crassly, spoiled kids demand to have things their way. A well-behaved adult masks the disturbing antics of the spoiled child, but our feelings indict us as people of privilege. Test this for yourself by reflecting on your feelings the last time a normal lifestyle object was taken away (e.g., a lost cell phone or a mechanical breakdown).

How does this privilege issue connect to the nitty-gritty issues of team? Team members bring a privileged view of life to the team. Team members may hesitate to give up a place of privilege to become one who serves others and the goals of the team.

Philippians 2 is the most significant Scripture on the idea of sharing power in teams. Jesus is described in verses 5–8 as the ultimate example of letting go of power. The original word describing Jesus' decision to leave heaven and fulfill his purpose on earth is *kenosis,* or "emptying out"; the ability to let go of something, especially if you have full right and privilege to hold on to that item. Jesus was the model of the ability to let go of a place in heaven to take the role of a man and to then offer his human life for a painful death for the benefit of the human race.

Americans find it hard to *step down* from a traditional level of comfort to a lower level (e.g., big house to little house). Whatever the level of comfort, there is a resistance to the downward movement. Power works the same way. What are you holding on to that you could not relinquish? What if we let go of our need to be right? How about releasing our need to take control of a situation in order to validate who we are? The challenge for us is to let go of our place of privilege so that we can fulfill a mission—a team outcome.

Think about privileges that a team member *might* need to let go for the team. Here's a list for reflection:

Favorite idea
Meeting time
Speaking time at meeting
Weekend
Membership on a sub-group of the team
Affirmation from others
Chief honcho image
Competitive drive
Budget authority
Hiring power
Final number crunching
Irrelevant stories
Historical tradition
(Add your own)

The Power in Two Versus One

Team is a value, a belief that one alone is not sufficient for many endeavors. Have you ever tried to hang a heavy kitchen cabinet by yourself? You simply need that second or third set of hands. Cooperation at times is a necessity. The benefit of team goes beyond necessity or efficiency. Teamwork done well is graceful and magical moving beyond necessity; a dynamic dance of exerting power and relinquishing power.

One of my passions is to participate in expeditionary outdoor travel. Expeditionary travel is done with small teams. The participants are the most important ingredient in putting together an expedition. The people on the journey are more important than the destination. Where one goes is important, but the dynamic of team and camaraderie becomes the central part of those experiences. Team has a human relationship payout that goes beyond the attainment of results—as important as that achievement might be.[2] Two is better than one.

Reasonable Self–Denial: Doormats Don't Really Share Power

Human doormats don't really share power. The sharing of power is based in choice, not in abdication. Dutifully serving as a doormat for anyone to walk on is not genuine sharing of power. To share power presumes a level of awareness of personal power. True sharing comes from the recognition of what *I can or could do* and my choice to defer to others' abilities and wishes. A solid team member looks at his own interests and at the interests of the others. "Do to others what you would have them do to you" is the familiar golden rule (Mt. 7:12). You must be spiritually alive to understand your personal needs and desires and to be willing to bring others' needs up to the same level of importance. A spiritually healthy individual knows her strengths and capacities. Cooperation is not abdication of personal power; it is intentional giving of my power to your presence. A doormat makes a poor team member because he has great difficulty making genuine contributions.

Reasonable self-denial is the key to sharing power. Deferring to others is a balancing act. If I accommodate endlessly then I have no strength of character and soul. Submitting to others in all circumstances is certainly not the model of Jesus at his trial and crucifixion. Intentional submission is healthy. Mindless submission creates two types of troubled souls. Unthinking self-denial can sap all the strength of soul and leave an empty chamber—a fragile and hollow person with little sense of self. Other times, people may submit only through coercion or obligation (perceived or real), and the seeds of bitterness and discontent are planted. Weeks or perhaps years later a volcanic explosion occurs. Severe explosions create damage to the mountain as well as the bystanders.

Snakes: The Dark Side of Power Abuse

Snakes get a bad rap because of a few deadly members of the family. But almost everyone feels creepy about snakes, so let's continue the unfair stereotype to describe a type of sinister team member. "Snakes" misuse positional power (e.g., team leader) or traditional power in the team to promote their own self-interests. Snakes should not be on teams because their power distortions will create no positive outcomes. Either quickly or over a longer period of time, snakes will poison the team. Snakes are not just an inconvenience; their power plays will destroy teams if not handled properly.

Slavery was always a bad idea because one human being assumed power over another based on nothing except a role or characteristic. Even *kind* slave owners were morally bankrupt because the power violated the essential equality of human beings. Sharing power in teams is not based on total equality, as in the case of human equality. But when power is disproportionately captured and then exercised capriciously, there cannot be shared power. The moral failure follows the same logic as in slavery. The concept of team becomes morally corrupted at that juncture.

Some snakes exhibit overt power like a bully demanding compliance. Other types of snakes will subvert the team atmosphere through conspiracy and subtle manipulation. The snake team member may appear to be with the program, but internally he is seething with the need to take power and is actively seeking to undermine the team through political maneuvers. Tactics such as these are unacceptable and the team will need to confront the deceptive behavior.

The best way to handle snakes is in the selection process. If you are involved in the initial selection of a team, by all means keep the snakes off the team. If you consider joining a team by invitation (as in a job change), test for snake behavior. As an outdoor enthusiast I've had several encounters with rattlesnakes through the years. Rattlesnakes seldom have reason for striking an unsuspecting hiker. Stepping on the snake becomes a good reason from the snake's perspective. A regular experience for a hiker is that of hearing the rattler announce its presence prior to seeing the snake. Rather than getting bitten, you get a warning. The rattle noise jumps your heart to your throat, and leg muscles launch you to a destination away from the noise of the snake. Both hiker and snake are happy about this arrangement, as the direct engagement was of little interest to either party. So it is with keeping a snake off a team. Both team and snake are better off. Those who select team members should listen for the distinct sound of the "rattling tail." Snakes provide the warning sound of the rattle because of the vibration in the ground from your approach. Stomp around a bit as you select a team. Communicate your expectations, check references about prospects, and listen well for the snakes rattling. Let them slither off to other endeavors as the team goes in an entirely different direction. Highly dysfunctional people should not be on high performance teams.

5

The Coach's Toolbox

Power Tools to Encourage Sharing Power

Warning Label: Disclaimers, Limitations, and Other Important Stuff

Great coaches are like skilled artisans who select the best tools to get the job done. The tool really needs to fit the job. The toolbox sections that follow list a number of tools that can be used to coach team members on both the spiritual *and* functional dimensions of team. The brief tool description provides information for the team coach to understand the potential use of each tool.

Tools can be misused. Putting the wrong tool into service at the wrong time always has the potential for messing things up on the team. Experimentation, on the other hand, can be a great learning time for coaches and for teams. So, have at it, use common sense, but do not use tools with reckless abandon. Remember the law of the hammer: give a young boy a hammer and soon you discover that everything was made for pounding. Here are a few other footnotes about tools in the hands of team coaches and team members.

1. Each toolbox chapter provides some general discussion and/ or tools on a major spiritual formation method available: Reflection, POG, Stories, Habits, Challenge, and Mystical Experiences.

2. Most tools are more specific and describe a personal or team exercise designed to assist in sharing power, creating positive climate, achieving results, and providing team energy.
3. One of the ways to classify tools is either as a reflective learning opportunity based in direct experiences or as a skill development exercise. Tools are categorized and coded as EL for Experiential Learning and SD for Skill Development.

Experiential Learning (EL) is a structured experience that is intended to lead to a new insight for an individual or the team. The insight could be related to one of the three types of gaps discussed in the section on Gapology in chapter 2. The new insight could focus on a functional or spiritual dimension of team. Experiential discovery tools are pre-planned by the coach with specific outcomes in mind.

Skill Development (SD) is a structured experience that is intended to bolster a specific skill. The physical skill of driving a car can be broken down into several sub-skills such as the look, the accelerator, the brake, and the turn. In a similar way, the SD exercise is intended to practice a key team skill to increase effectiveness. A great team returns to skill development to impact their overall effectiveness.

4. The author's clear bias is that these tools be used for self-directed teams. The coaching tools are great for an *external coach or facilitator*. External coaches have an important role in early team development and later on as occasional resources. In the self-directed team the external coach's role is quickly replaced by the model of skilled team members who share coaching and leadership roles.

Spiritual Formation Tools for Sharing Power

Tool # 1—The Path of Personal Reflection (EL)

Building bridges across the gaps in our lives is the heart of spiritual growth, as discussed in chapter 2. Reflection is a classic tool in spiritual formation that can be applied to the issue of sharing power or other spiritual team dimensions. Here are a few observations about leveraging reflection as a useful tool to move team members to greater growth.

Choose to Create Reflection in Your Life

The greatest challenge to reflection is not the capacity for thinking but the opportunity to think in today's lifestyle. People today go from face-to-face dialogue to cell phone conversations to email to iPod to TV to bed to wake-up via radio, and the cycle begins again. The constant auditory and visual stimulation coupled with ever-increasing demands for productivity have eliminated reflection from many lives.

As a team leader, create reflection space to work on the big picture problems of your team-based organization as well as your personal life. Simple ideas include: solo drive time with no noise, TV disconnection, and a traditional quiet time that opens the door for prayer and deep thinking. Spend three days totally alone and discover all kinds of spiritual issues. Tool # 4 offers some suggestions for solitude retreats.

Hire a personal coach to help you work on reflecting. The reflection imbedded in the coaching conversation is fundamental to the coaching process. Reflection is enhanced in solitude, but dialogical reflection can be equally powerful. The coaching process asks powerful questions. The goal of powerful questions is to push us to a deeper level of thought: "I don't know. I'll need to think on that one for awhile," is an honest answer to a great question. The Hebrew meaning for the word *meditation* is to roll something over again and again. Deep thoughts are complicated: "The purposes of a man's heart are deep waters, but a man of understanding draws them out" (Prov. 20:5). Coaches push for reflection in their clients.

Reflection is not the same as introspection. Introspection is a reflective process that moves to a world of inner voices and thoughts as the sole source of reflection. Introspection is one type of input, but not the exclusive diet of reflection. The inner world is seen through the lens of our unique personality with all its strengths and all its flaws. Reflection should be multi-dimensional and include input or thoughts from a number of sources. The Bible is our key companion for Christian reflection because of its importance as a different voice—different from the voice of introspection. Scripture's voice can be true and trustworthy, stern or comforting as the Holy Spirit speaks through it.

Input from others is another strand of information in the reflection model. Team member feedback provides a different thought stream than the solitary voice found in introspection. Coaches can provide helpful feedback as well. Find a personal coach who is a true encourager and who is also willing to take risks of providing strong feedback for your reflection. Leaders need truth-teller data to counteract the negligible information provided by most friends and colleagues. Personal reflection in its many forms is a tool that moves us further down the path of spiritual development.

Tool #2—*Soften Your View (EL)*

Write down your three most stubborn positions (political, family, religious) in your journal and see if you can soften them in the weeks ahead.

A group version of this exercise directs team members to identify a part of life where they want to be more flexible and teachable. The area for change could be anything: something in the work setting, a stereotype about octogenarians, or a fiercely held theological belief.

Tool # 3—*Listening for Value Exercise (SD)*

One way to increase your capacity for sharing is to see the value represented in other team members. At one of the next team meetings, listen carefully to each team member with the intent of identifying key values each member brings to the team. After the meeting, enter in your journal what you heard specifically and each person's value and contribution to the team. Perhaps you heard a teammate share insight on the consequences of a project decision on clerical staff. Upon reflection you characterize her as someone who is great at providing the impact-on-people viewpoint.

If the team has a longer history, make a member-contributions list in the journal prior to the team meeting. After listening at the team meeting, review the list and see what new things might be added to the strengths each person brings.

Tool # 4—*Extended Time for Reflection through Solitude (SD/EL)*

Team and solo might seem to be contradictory concepts, but that is not necessarily so. Dietrich Bonhoeffer was a German theologian who died at the hands of the Nazi's because of his leadership in the resistance movement. He makes the bold statement in *Life Together*[1] that only in knowing solitude and being alone can one contribute to community.

The role of solitude and reflection builds team because it closes personal spiritual gaps (Types I–III). The person with greater spiritual health is in a better place to make contributions to team and community. Here are suggestions for one-day and three-day solo experiences.

Make Preparations

Where to go and what to bring: Find a place of *necessary minimal comforts* (somewhere between a tent and a one-star hotel, depending on who you are). If you have the opportunity for a setting that includes access to serene outdoor space, that would be a great plus. Leave behind the MEDS (modern electronic diversionary systems) such as TV and iPod. Wear comfortable clothes for sitting and walking. Bring a journal and some key reflective materials, such as your Bible. Reflective material might also include some notes from past coaching sessions, a self-assessment inventory, or a key devotional classic.

One-Day Design

Get to your place of retreat in time to eat supper and then devote the evening to reflection activities. Reflection involves thinking, journaling, and reading Scripture. Start the evening with a journal entry asking some broad questions: What are the expectations or hopes that you bring to the solo time? What key questions do you want to ponder? Set aside some time to reflect on what key events have occurred in your life since the last solo experience. Summarize what the key events have brought to your life in terms of insights and understanding. Are these issues just coming on the radar screen now, or recycled from previous times?

Rank your reflection issues in terms of which ones seem to have the greatest energy. Then rank the list again for those that have the potential for the greatest impact on your life—either negative or positive impact. The goal in the opening reflection is to focus on life issues. In the words of Thomas Merton, "Meditation has no point and no reality unless it is firmly rooted in *life*."[2]

Before you finish for the night, read more Scripture, take a page in the journal and write the word *"Surprises"* as a title, leaving some open space below. Regardless of what one brings as a purpose or goal, there will always be surprises. Surprises are like teachable moments. One can't plan or predict a teachable moment, or surprises (obviously), but a readiness for surprises enables you to see them when they arrive.

The next morning, eat breakfast. Spend some time writing in your journal. Ask yourself some powerful questions about the issues outlined the night before. Here is a list of some questions to consider.

- What part of that issue would you like to focus on during this solo?
- What do you want?
- What do others in the situation want?
- If you had a magic wand and could instantly create a new reality, what would it look like?
- What is standing in your way?
- What other options are you considering?
- Who can I ask to help me bring a different perspective to this venture?
- How would you summarize the actions you plan to take?

After some reflection, go for a walk. Rest or take a nap if you feel tired. Reflection is usually not about the quantity of thinking as much as the quality.

Have some lunch. Spend additional time reading, writing, and thinking. Scribble, draw, or doodle if you are a visual thinker. Walk. Finish the afternoon with a clear focus on prescriptive action steps that are attainable and have specific time frames for action. Depart for home. Enjoy your dinner. Share key insights and action plans with a key friend or colleague.

Three-Day Design

The key difference between a one-day solo and a three-day solo is the inability to escape your self. Strategies to avoid self and deeper issues become much less successful on extended solo.

Follow the schedule suggested for the one-day solo with the variation of adding longer periods of rest and walking and reflection.

Tool # 5—Fasting—Nurturing the Power to Defer (EL/SD)

Fasting is the most practical form of developing reasonable self-denial. The human body wants food regularly and often obsessively. Fasting is a simple, direct way to practice reasonable self-denial. Health professionals advocate fasting for physical benefits alone. At a spiritual level, an individual is immediately in touch with the choice to defer desires. I'm hungry! Do I grab that donut in the conference room or do I maintain my fast? I make a choice to deny myself or to satisfy my cravings.

The classic spiritual fast presents a great parallel with teamwork. In a team I defer my interests to a larger goal—it's not about me but the team purpose. In a spiritual fast there is also a purpose. It might be quite personal, such as reconnecting with the Spirit of God or listening for a key life decision. The purpose might be to pray for a church or a country or any number of possibilities beyond myself. When fasting I submit my will (desires) to a larger purpose.

Fast once a week as a lifestyle practice. The simple fast begins after supper and involves eating no solid foods the rest of the evening or the next day until sundown. Drink plenty of water. Set aside the time typically allocated for meals to instead do prayer and reflection. A person practiced in fasting is more prepared to perform healthy self-denial and to share power in a team.

Consider a team fast. Determine a key result that the team is pursuing, such as a new plan or achieving a positive outcome from a scheduled event. Team members agree to set aside a specific day (or days) to fast. Process the reflections from the fast at a team meeting.

Tools for Improving the Functional Dimensions of Sharing Power in Team

Tool # 6—*Voice as Key Indicator for Assessing Power in Teams (EL)*

A self-directed team needs all of its members to understand the four basic functional dimensions of team and be able to maintain a perpetual assessment of the function. A key indicator for each dimension helps team members pay attention to that function. *Voice is the key indicator of power dynamics in a team.* As previously discussed, the issue of voice is partly quantitative and partly qualitative. Team members need to be heard, and a critically important tool for leadership is to observe the sharing of voice as the key indicator of sharing of power. Observe communication in the team and listen for equality in voice. Do several team members dominate? Are opinions and observations valued around the team meeting table? Voice is not the only indicator of power sharing, but does represent a key symptom of the power dynamics.

Tool # 7—*Rounds Encourage Voice Equality (SD)*

One of the simplest interventions for voice equality is the technique of sharing by round. As a decision-making conversation has progressed and is moving to a conclusion, leadership creates a check-in question: "Let's test where we are on the topic of converting to high deductible health care and personal insurance accounts. Starting with Mary[3] and moving to her right, everyone gets two sentences to summarize their position." The round creates a firm structure to acknowledge everyone's voice of influence for the group. The time to do a round can be shortened from an invitation for short comments to more definitive responses to a closed question. "It seems like we are moving to a consensus on the new youth center location on 5th Street. On a scale of 1–10, with 10 being highly supportive and 1 being highly unsupportive, what number would you assign? George, let's begin with you." The question could also be framed for a "Yes or No," an "In or Out," or some other kind of short response. Pick a quick processor to get the round started rather than one of the slow processors.

Tool # 8—The Trump Card Dialogue (EL)

One of the most important conversations for any team is to talk about how decisions are made and who makes what kinds of decisions. A simple way to coach this conversation uses cards. The discussion is framed with an overview of decision-making in teams. There are two issues to be discussed: the "how to decide" and "what can be decided by the team." The "how" is best tackled first. When our team is empowered to make a decision, how will we make the decision? An outline as illustrated in the table below can provide a framework for discussion. The team can discuss how such strategies empower or handicap the team.

Absolute consensus	Principled consensus	Democratic votes	Autocratic veto
Everyone agrees on every decision before the group	Consensus pursued with members willing to defer	A majority vote (simple or predetermined ratio)	Team decides, but positional leader may veto

After defining the range of options, the team can discuss the pros and cons of the various methods. The consensus model described in chapter 3 provides additional resources for teaching the team about consensus.

The second point of discussion is clarification of the limits of team empowerment: What decisions can or cannot be made by the team? The organization at large or a key staff member present on the team must decide which trump cards will be held by "someone."

A trump card can overrule a team decision or sentiment. You may use Post-it® notes to symbolize the trump cards.

Tool # 9—The Incomplete Bridge (EL)

Briefing: Teaching through metaphor can be a helpful way to introduce a new topic. "Incomplete Bridge" is an initiative game that can be both fun and instructional. Team members are told that the incomplete bridge activity is an opportunity to explore how teams make decisions and exercise power. Those not familiar with this type of experiential learning exercise should consult our Web site for important principles for coaching an experiential learning exercise (www.spirituallyhealthyteams.com).

Props: "Big Bridges" is the most traditional version of "Incomplete Bridge" and involves some props that are set-up in the following manner. A video clip of this event is available on the Web site mentioned above for the visual learners. A tabletop version of the exercise, called "Golden Gate," is available and uses toy cars and bridge spans. The following props are needed for "Big Bridges":

- Two 48" x 48" platforms
- One 24" x 24" platform
- One 2" x 6" board 7 feet long
- One 2" x 6" board 3 feet long

Pallets make an inexpensive substitute for platforms rather than building your own. Not all pallets are created equal. Avoid big gaps in your platforms. The platforms are arranged in a line starting with one large platform, a space of approximately 100 inches from the edge of the large platform to the edge of the smaller (24" x 24") platform, followed by another space of 100 inches from the further edge of the smaller platform to the edge of the second large platform.

Objectives: The team is assembled on the first platform and must move across the open spaces between the platforms. The team must move with only the aid of the two planks and the problem-solving resources of the team. The platforms cannot be moved. The initiative event can be framed simply or perhaps woven into a fanciful tale. The team is a part of a rescue effort that has now come to the Baby Nile River and must cross to the other side using only the small island (the small platform) and planks to accomplish their task. Success, of course, will mean having saved starving children with food and medical supplies carried by the team.

Rules: The following rules are important to make sure the initiative game remains a true challenge. Two planks are available for the group to use. If the planks touch the rapidly moving water they are lost for the crossing, which means failure. However, the coach of the exercise frequently chooses to offer the group the choice to start again after recovering the planks from downstream. Platforms must be spaced properly. No running jumps between platforms—only stepping allowed.

Debriefing: As the team comes to a successful resolution of the Big Bridge exercise, craft several questions to allow team members to reflect on the learning event. The process of sharing ideas for solutions to the problem reflects the equal or unequal power of voice in the team. Here are a few examples of reflection questions.

- How would you evaluate the sharing of the decision-making during this event?
- How much equality of voice did we exhibit?
- Assuming the team got to the breakthrough idea of using the boards as simple levers: How much change in the position of the lever did it take to make a difference in function? What parallels did you see between the use of levers in solving this problem and the sharing of power in team?
- What ways did you maximize the resources of all team members?

Tool # 10—Assessing Power Distribution through Post-it® Notes (EL)

The cycle for a positive launch of a team is briefly discussed in chapter 15. Early events, such as building the team contract and discussion of decision-making method will clarify expectations for the team's sharing of power. Once the team has been working together for some time, it's a good idea to do a routine check-up on how the power distribution is functioning within the team. This assessment exercise is a handy way to explore that distribution. Observable issues around power sharing within the group may also prompt the use of this exercise.

The Post-it® note process uses behavioral indicators of power to assess the relative value given to the input of team members. Relative inequality of power within groups should be expected. Some members always hold greater influence within a team. One issue is whether that inequality is based on respect and talent or whether the inequality is based on a team member's attempts to grasp power by virtue of role or ego. Power dimensions tend to be recycled around different issues in the group. The characters and story line are the same; the contextual issue is different. Most team members have a general sense of their position of influence within the group.

Assess the overall power grid with this group feedback process. An open and honest process is essential. A spiritually immature team is a dangerous place to do this analysis. Two variations of this process are available. One provides a simpler report and the other a more complex reporting of the team data and dynamics. The simpler approach is called the One-Degree Post-it exercise and the more complicated approach is called the 360-Degree Post-it because of its similarity with a 360-degree leadership assessment process. Visit our Web site for the description of the 360-degree evaluation process.

The One-Degree Post-it® Power Note:

Begin by reminding the group how the level of voice is a key indicator for power. Remind the team of its commitment to be

---

Post-it® Power Note

My voice is a _____in this group

10 = heard and valued equally with others
1 = not heard & valued equally with others

---

honest in feedback and conversations. Each person is given a Post-it note pre-printed with this question and asked to respond with a number from 1 to 10. Alternatively, one could write the question on a flipchart and provide a blank Post-it® note for each person in the team

Provide a minute or so for the team members to complete the notes, having told them that notes will be collected and will anonymously be posted to the flipchart. Since an open discussion of power is one of the most sensitive topics in teams, I prefer to start with the anonymity instruction and then provide opportunity later for increased level of self-disclosure. In a very healthy team that has good history and vitality, the anonymity step can be skipped.

Collect the notes and post them on the flipchart or white board. A coaching question could be, "As you observe the notes and their numbers, what does that indicate for the team's ability to share power?" The analytics will want to repost the notes into a linear arrangement with low numbers on the left and high numbers to the right.

Different issues will surface according to the group's life. Some classics include: Does the power grid need to have all nines and tens? What is the level of comfort or discontent with the distribution? What are the feelings attached to those who may have offered lower numbers (1–3)?

The key issue in this exercise is to ask questions about power inequities (if they exist) because power is about perception. Make sure that action plans coming from the discussion are behavioral in nature. What did the group do in the past to discourage empowerment, and, more importantly, what practices can be put in place to encourage empowerment? For example, the team may conclude that one key member is so forceful in style that this person often "runs over" two other members who are reticent to speak. Keep any discussion on the past away from the blame game. Consider past behavior only long enough for the team to "get it." Push the focus to the future and what specific actions can be done to encourage more equitable sharing of power. Teams may choose to implement new habits, such as a better check-in prior to decisions or to humorously remind Fred he is doing his domineering thing again and needs to yield the floor.

6

Achieving Results in Teams

The Parable of the Ants and the Unmovable Rock

At the bottom of a bluff in the deserts of southern California there were two colonies of ants. Each colony had a well-established ant hole—some ants build down under the ground rather than build up into anthills. One day the ground began to shake with a large earthquake. The shaking ground dislodged several rocks at the top of the bluff and the rocks came crashing down the side of the hill. Talk about bad luck—each colony ended up with a big rock smack dab on the top of its ant-hole entrance. Hundreds of ants were trapped inside but those ants on the outside of their ant homes formed two rescue teams. Each colony's rescue team faced what appeared to be an impossible task. How would the rescue team move such a large rock and free their colony? As you know, ants are very strong—lifting over twenty times their body weight. Ants are also very hard workers. But what would it take for the teams to move the seemingly unmovable rocks?

One rescue team, whom we'll call the White Team, immediately tried to push the rock out of the way. At first they did not succeed, so of course they tried and tried again. Ants are experts at moving things and applied all their traditional lifting and pulling techniques. Each attempt was valiant but unsuccessful. As other wandering ants came back to the colony entrance, the team would enlist their help, but even the larger team could not move the rock because it was too heavy. Finally, exhausted and depleted they collapsed in defeat around the rock.

The rescue team from the second colony will be known as the Green Team. The Green Team ants were very hard workers and very strong just like the White Team. But the Green Team was also very creative. After exploring the problem, they concluded that the traditional lift and pull techniques would not work on such a large rock. Thinking creatively, new ideas started to emerge from the different members of the rescue team. New ideas led to analysis, which led to a decision to move forward with the idea with the greatest potential.

The Green Team assembled all its members and began the trek to the top of the bluff—which took an hour of rapid hiking. The creative team had determined the type of rock on top of their home appeared to be a shale rock. Too big to move but maybe not too big to break! At the top of the bluff the ants found several smaller rocks that they could move. Push, push, and a stone went over the edge. The stone went cascading down the hill and missed its intended target. So the Green Team tried again and then again. On the fourth try the stone from above hit the shale rock below and they cheered loudly. The brittle shale rock was now broken into half a dozen pieces. The ants quickly descended the bluff, and with great fervor and persistence moved the shale fragments away from the covered ant hole. The rest of the colony was now free and there was a great celebration. The ants had moved the unmovable rock and the colony went on to a long and prosperous life together.

There is a lot to be learned from the difference between the Green Team and the White Team of ants in their attempts to move the rocks. Those who want to understand about teams should listen carefully to the teamwork secrets demonstrated by the Green Team in getting the job done.

The Parable Interpretation

Every team has a rock to move: a project, a desired outcome, a goal to achieve. If there is not an objective, then there is only a group and not a team. The question is, How do we *move the rock*? How do we most effectively get the job done and achieve the desired results? Highly effective teams approach their problems like the Green Team, who in moving the rock demonstrated a creative process that involved all the resources of the team. Rather than depend strictly on the strategies of the past or on known strengths and expertise, they were able to be creative. The most challenging part of the problem-solving process is creating the ideas that will address the real problems that teams face. A variety of techniques can be used to help draw out the creative potential of the entire team. Once a team has creative ideas, it must continue with other kinds of heavy lifting in order to metaphorically move the rock. The skill of solving problems involves heavy lifting, such as analysis of ideas, consequential thinking, and sequential planning. Implementation, persistence, and adaption are all part of the pathway to final success and celebration. The Green Team exercised all of these functional skills, whereas the White Team remained stuck in the skills and strategies from their past. The Green Team succeeded and the White Team worked tirelessly but failed.

Four key dimensions of effectiveness create successful self-directed teams; two keys have now been revealed:

- *Share the power* (symbolized by balancing a stick)
- *Move the rock* (achieve team results symbolized by moving a rock)

Leadership in teams involves influencing the four key processes toward sustained effectiveness. A contract is the key statement of values that define who the team can become, and is a simple and powerful tool to regulate the team's character and performance.

Achieving Results as a Functional Dimension of Team

Achieving team outcomes or getting the job done is one of the four functional dimensions of team. Moving a rock is a metaphor for the fundamental work of the team. Every team has a purpose. The more vivid and specific that purpose, the easier it will be to focus on results. Moving the rock is the metaphor for the mechanics of the problem-solving process. This chapter provides a brief explanation of the central pieces teams need to get to results. Effective teams need strong skills in creative and critical thinking, planning and implementation, and efficient team meeting times to achieve team goals.

What differentiates a group from a team is that a team has specific results it is trying to achieve. There are many systems and models that help teams solve problems and achieve results. At the risk of oversimplification, one can reduce all these models into two big steps in the problem-solving process: the design side and the implementation side. A team needs to make a plan or design an answer to the problem facing them. A team also needs to implement the plan to achieve the desired results. Plan and execute. Design and implement. Create and produce. Hypothesize and experiment. Imagine and act. Terminology will change, but the two-step process remains the same.

Some teams focus more on the visionary or conceptual side of the divide. The team results are wrapped in the design of a possible outcome. Planning teams may hand off a major part of the implementation to other teams. Implementation or production teams specialize in get-it-done. A complicated implementation scheme repeats the same two-step process of planning how to implement and then doing it. The cycle continues. Better design of assessment strategies completes the circle. But it all begins again to improve every part of the process, to achieve more.

Most teams struggle to bring the creative resources necessary to solve the problem. True creativity is expressed in the totally new idea—or at least it seems new. New for the sake of new is not important, but new for the sake of creating a better way toward the vision is exciting. There is wisdom in the old country phrase, "If it ain't broke, don't fix it." Creativity is not about change for the sake of change, but change whenever it can produce a better result. Improve whatever can be improved. Focus on the parts that can make a difference. Creative change represents major leaps forward.

Creativity in teams is a skill that can be enhanced by a variety of systems. A common element in brainstorming, mind mapping, or playtime is to create time and a safe space for ideas to be generated. People take greater social risks and suggest new ideas in a context free of immediate criticism. The classic brainstorming technique invokes the rule of deferred judgment during the ideation phase of the process. As the ideas are created, the judgment of those ideas is suspended until later in the process. The strength of *The Six Thinking Hats* system by Ed DeBono is separation of different types of thinking into different time frames.[1] Strong analytical and consequential thinking (Black Hat) is done separately from the creative thinking times (Yellow Hat and Green Hat). Few people are willing to keep sharing ideas that are immediately rebuffed. Teams profit from systems that develop creative thinking skills.

Ideas also need time to incubate. Not every great idea happens in a moment of free association; they percolate to the surface over time. Creative thinking needs extra time to get to the best results. I hired a contractor who had run into some problems while excavating under a building that was going to be moved. He told me he'd be back in a day or so once he figured out what to do. Two days later he was back with a very creative and cost-effective solution.

Of course, creativity is only half the battle; strong skills in evaluation and analysis must be applied to sort out the best ideas. The discussion in chapter 7 speaks about the spiritual base in evaluation skills and the wisdom found in rigorous thinking. Teams also need what is called means-ends thinking. The goal is clear, the creative method or means is selected through analysis, and now the step-by-step sequence needs to be put in place. Crafting a detailed plan with the steps of implementation will round out the "get-'er-done" process. The whole package is what gets the team to its desired results. The toolbox in chapter 8 points to resources that help teams expand their creativity and analysis skills.

The first big step to getting great results is for a team to demonstrate the full range of powerful thinking; the second great challenge is to get all that good thinking and planning done efficiently in team meetings. The classic argument for team-based organizations is that seven minds are better than one mind, and more powerful thinking can result. The classic complaint against teams is that the process "kills" everyone. No one wants to sit through a long and boring team meeting filled with trivial talking, recitation of old stories, and not enough clear decision and action. The aversion to boring meetings is so high that many leaders will sacrifice the benefits of team to avoid the pain of meetings.

The meeting length itself is not the killer; rather, it is the use of a bad meeting process instead of a good process. The goal needs to be to balance effectiveness and efficiency. Effectiveness is achieving the desired result. Efficiency is achieving that result with the greatest return on the investment of time and other resources. Great meetings are essential to the team experience. The toolbox in chapter 8 outlines some strategies to keep team meetings on task and achieve results.

The high performance team develops all the skills necessary to get results. Planning skills represented by the capacity to think powerfully (creatively, critically, and sequentially) are foundational and represent a major functional dimension in teams. The team meeting becomes the laboratory where so much of this planning process takes place. How do we get there? How come team meetings can be so frustrating? Skilled people underperform; why is that? Surely part of the issue is skill development. Team members need rigorous training in these disciplines in the same way employees need training on computers or whatever technical skill is necessary to do specific work. But the functional skill sets are only part of the solution. The spiritual dimensions of solving problems are the key to successful team.

7

Spiritual Issues
of Moving the Rock

What are the spiritual dimensions that impact a team's ability to solve problems and achieve results? Is strategic thinking and strategic doing a matter of skills and intelligence and nothing about spirituality and attitudes? What we believe has a lot to say about our ability to think creatively, evaluate rigorously, and implement effectively.

One of the most exciting experiences for me is to be with a group of creative people trying to solve tough problems. One of the most miserable places to be is sitting in a meeting with people who have surrendered their opportunity to solve problems in exchange for complaints and inaction. Ministry teams should be the most creative, best-thinking, highest productivity teams on the planet. Here is why.

Cocreators with God

"For it is by grace you have been saved, through faith—and this not from yourselves, it is the gift of God—not by works, so that no one can boast. For we are God's workmanship, created in Christ Jesus to do good works, which God prepared in advance for us to do" (Eph. 2: 8–10). Your life has significance because God has a role for you to play while wandering the planet for the next eighty years or eight days depending on how long you have left. God is purposeful and has a plan for your life. God has created you and intends you to create good works as well.

God is the Creator or Designer. The majestic mountains or the desert expanse at sunset invokes wonder and appreciation. "Great are the works of the LORD, they are pondered by all who delight in them. Glorious and majestic are his deeds. And his righteousness endures forever" (Ps. 111:2–3). Paul the apostle wrote, "For since the creation of the world God's invisible qualities—his eternal power and divine nature—have been clearly seen, being understood from what has been made, so that men are without excuse" (Rom. 1:20). The art work is incredible. The artist is revealed by the work of art. God as the masterful artist did not limit himself to nature landscapes but can be seen in the beauty and mystery of each person.

Imago Dei means that people are created in the *image of God.* (Gen 1:26–27). Central to that image is our capacity for creation. Obviously we procreate physically, but parents also nurture children into responsible adults as part of a creative process. Most of our "work activity" is some form of creation, from the homes we build to the cars we drive to the backyard garden. We are all potential designers, some more smitten by the creative bug than others.

All children show design capacity by the play spaces they create when given some wood and string and perhaps a hammer and a few nails. As a kid I remember fondly the hours spent as a civil engineer creating dams in the rural creek that ran behind the barn. The fun and hard work of trying to slow the water and create a pond upstream were entertainment for an afternoon. Sand castles, bedroom forts from extra sheets, or decorated cookies all point to the childhood desire to create.

God runs a codesign operation that is an expression of one of the great paradoxes of faith: sovereignty versus free will. God created the universe and is in control and yet invites us to participate in the next great design operation. God somehow limits himself to work through you and me in this world and yet is not limited by you and me at all—the paradox. Paradox is when two truths that appear to be in opposition to one another are viewed as equally true at the same time. Paradox is both/and rather than either/or. Our role as cocreator is a paradox. God is expecting you and me to create. The future for your church organization and the kingdom of God depends on the creativity of your team. Yet you cannot thwart the ultimate purposes of God the Creator—no way, not ever.

Hiding in the sovereignty side of the paradox leads people to abdicate their role as cocreator. Failure to accept the responsibility as a cocreator is extremely dangerous spiritually. The familiar parable of the talents outlines God's expectation that you and your team achieve outcomes (Mt. 25:14–28). The harsh judgment in the parable acknowledges the paradox and then sends the do-nothing servant (say ministry team) to hell.

> His master replied, "You wicked, lazy servant! So you knew that I harvest where I have not sown and gather where I have not scattered seed? Well then, you should have put my money on deposit with the bankers, so that when I returned I would have received it back with interest. Take the talent from him and give it to the one who has the ten talents. For everyone who has will be given more, and he will have an abundance. Whoever does not have, even what he has will be taken from him. And throw that worthless servant outside, into the darkness, where there will be weeping and gnashing of teeth." (Mt. 25: 26–28)

The creativity agenda for teams begins with accepting our responsibility and opportunity to be cocreators with God for his work here on earth. Creativity is both a great invitation and a duty. Step into your role as a cocreator with enthusiasm. Act as though the salvation of the world depends on the work of your team—which of course is true. And of course God alone saves the world, through faith and even that is a gift from God—the paradox.

So what are the spiritual roadblocks that keep us from fulfilling our creative mandate? A number of things get in the way of teams achieving results. Here are three negative attitudes that ministry teams encounter. Confront them and enable the team to replace the roadblocks with the spiritually positive alternative: freedom from tradition (a new thing), freedom from busyness (a new focus), and freedom from fear (a new courage).

Freedom from Tradition—Freedom for a New Thing

All tradition starts as good tradition—right? Or else why would it become a tradition? Take the tradition of boiling water before drinking. Removing harmful parasites that would do damage to your body is a good idea. Boiling water to purify it is referenced in cultures before the invention of the microscope. The microscope and scientific experiments later confirmed why boiling was so important to our health. Water purification made a major leap with the micron filter. With the same objective for healthy water a sophisticated technology has replaced a primitive one. Micron filters have holes so small that molecules of water will pass through the screen but the single-cell parasite will get trapped.

What moves us from a tradition proven valuable in the past and allows us to go down a different path? How do you let go of boiling water and invent the micro screen? Boiling water is not a bad idea, but micro screens are a superior idea in certain contexts. There is no bigger issue in the church today than the need to extract the purpose from a tradition so that the purpose can still be met and the older method can be left behind. But the challenge is nothing new, as we see in Isaiah 43:18–19, "Forget the former things; do not dwell on the past. See, I am doing a new thing! Now it springs up; do you not perceive it? I am making a way in the desert and streams in the wasteland." God wants us to do something new. God wants us to create new things with him, and yet most of us are stuck in traditions that need to be left behind.

The church has become increasingly irrelevant to average folks in the community because the church has become isolated from culture and walks predominantly in its traditions. Team-based ministry organizations can be creative in these changing times. Creativity will always run into tradition, and often loses. New for the sake of newness has little value. Yet great value exists when important purposes are achieved because of new and more effective methods.

Most people think that "other people" are rich. People follow similar justification to identify who is stuck in tradition—those people are stuck, not me. Each team member brings a wealth of life experience to the team. A team member will often eliminate a new idea for the team because of a personal tradition. If the team member's life includes a bad experience with some fund-raising event, then that negative tradition will be raised at the team's suggestion of a similar fund-raising strategy. Although life experience should be a teacher for the future, how presumptuous that everything suggested by others be evaluated through my limited life filter.

How do I break free of my traditional views? Begin by adopting a larger frame of reference—get over yourself and your past experiences. Your life experience is valuable, but it is also limited. In the world of prejudice reduction is an important idea called *individualization of negative experience.* Many people have a significant negative experience with a person from a different social or ethnic group. The problem arises because that single experience is then broadened as a judgment of the entire social group. Just because one man treated me poorly does not mean that all men will treat me poorly. Overcome your own limited experiences in life by realizing that some of your negative experiences with projects or ideas were unique experiences. As a team member do not let your previous experience kill new ideas. Be open to ideas based on their inherent potential and rigorous evaluation. Been-there-done-that perspectives can be helpful but often are tragic killers in the problem-solving process.

Bad experiences can get elevated to a status not deserved, and good experiences can be just as limiting to a team. The *good-ole-days* attitude is another limiting belief that can stifle new thinking and new creation. There is no doubt that pieces of the good ole days should be preserved. The question is which piece is a tradition worth preservation. Guard carefully what should be preserved.

The test for tradition is found in the principle, not the prescription. Respect for teachers is a critical principle for quality education. Having all students stand at attention at their desk when a teacher enters the room is a specific prescriptive behavior to show respect—and debatable as a tradition in the modern classroom. The prescription is variable but the principle is essential. When teams create new methods to achieve a traditional principle or goal, the focus needs to remain pragmatic—how will this work? If it works, it accomplished the outcome. Methods and ideas will change. Team members must escape the traps of both good and bad traditions. The toolbox in chapter 8 outlines a few practices that encourage the team member to develop the *new-thing* way of thinking and to be genuinely free from tradition. God is interested in doing a new thing; how about your team?

Freedom from Busyness—Freedom for a New Focus

Teams are either voluntary or involuntary. Most teams in the work place are involuntary. Most teams in churches are filled with volunteers. Volunteer teams have a greater time shortage issue than work teams. Producing results on volunteer teams is derailed because assignments simply don't get done by team members. Life happens. The volunteer duty usually falls below other duties in the priority matrix of day job, shuttling children, and fixing dinner.

Showing Up: "Eighty percent of success is showing up" is a quote widely attributed to Woody Allen. Volunteer teams need to create systems that help them *show up* to do the work after the team meeting is over. Here are a few ideas.

- There are no easy answers to this challenge except maybe blowing up your TV.[1]
- The group can become a motivational tool to help team members complete the task (see POG—chapter 10).
- Use specific due dates on assignments.
- No one wants to be nagged, but many people do step up when reminded via phone or e-mail or personal note about the to-do list. Teams can set up check-in meetings via conference call. Keep it encouraging, not punitive and judgmental.
- More powerful than accountability approaches is *the impact of visionary commitment* to help volunteers *show up*. Commitment is a deep certainty in the object of our belief. Action will flow from that deep resolve.
- Restate the vision—again and again and again and again. Make the vision specific. Talk about how great it will be when... Reframe the vision as a story or compelling word picture that speaks about the need.
- High fives. Find success and celebrate in the team meeting when things go right. Take every opportunity available to celebrate team movement toward the vision.
- Individual coaching is a great method for helping a volunteer team get things done. Who does the coaching? A self-directed team trained in coaching methodology could develop a peer coaching system between members. But an external coach (someone not on the team) has some advantages because they are not a part of the current team culture.

Freedom from Fear—Freedom for New Courage

Large organizations and their teams can suffer from a lack of creativity that stems from fear. If I get into trouble by speaking up or by pointing to the unnamed elephant in the room, I will not risk creativity in team problem solving. Fear limits creativity. Organizations that lead through fear and silence dwarf the creative potential of their teams.

Within the team, members fear rejection. Fear of rejection can reside in a generally weak sense of self and a disbelief in competence. Teams need to encourage courage. Be courageous. Think differently.

Imagine that creativity is central to your team process. Imagination is not just an opportunity to solve problems but an energizing behavior. Teams where members look forward to solving the problems are exciting places to work and live. Some of you have had that great experience of being a part of one of those groups. Others are hoping to be in one of those teams soon.

The teams that achieve their creative potential assume their cocreative role with God. These teams have great technique and skill but they have also pushed past common blockades to imagination. Team members are committed to achieving the results of the team and show up to do the work. There is a noticeable freedom from tradition and a lack of institutional fear, so people are willing to take risks, make mistakes, and offer up an idea that may become the launching pad for greatness.

Why Christians Don't Think

Critical Examination

Teams can suffer from a lack of creative thinking. Ministry teams can also suffer from a lack of critical examination. But critical thinking has an indispensable role. Every creative plan or creative idea needs to be evaluated. Great teams need to exercise the ability to rigorously evaluate possibilities.

There is an interesting belief among some in the church that evaluation is not a spiritual enterprise. The belief goes something like this: "God gave me/us a great idea. God will take care of everything. If the plan is from God then everything will take care of itself. The budget problem—oh, that is only a matter of lack of faith. It will be God's miracle. Believe in the miraculous." A miracle is when something happens outside of the regular norm. Something extraordinary or a change in the timing of an event is miraculous. A miracle is something that, by its nature, is an exception to a natural law that God has created. I once fell from a height that would ordinarily kill someone. I consider the fact that I survived a minor miracle, as it seemed to be an exception to the forces of gravity. There are laws of nature that control falling and heat transfer and energy conversion. There are also laws of the marketplace and laws of business and leadership and so forth. Most of the time, life unfolds according to the natural laws of God. Evaluation or critical thinking involves testing for consistencies with God's natural law.

Let me give you an example. Retail business people use the phrase, "Location, location, location." The clear law of the market is that your place of business is extremely important. Success in a traditional retail market is predicated on being near your customers. If one store has great merchandise, great prices, a great location, and the friendliest staff on earth, sales will be higher than the enterprise that has all of those entities but is in a poor location. There are exceptions, but the law is consistent. God could create a miracle and cause the store to prosper in an out-of-the-way place. However, when God gave them a creative idea for a storefront (being the source of all creativity), God wanted to bless them by having the storefront in the right location too.

Rigorous critical thinking is expressed most clearly in the wisdom literature of Scripture. The Proverbs are full of critical principles that serve as guides to all kinds of pursuits. The wisdom literature is one of the key places to discover the natural law of God. For example, hard work produces results, while being a slacker leads to ruin (Prov. 6:6–11).

Every action has consequences. When a leader foresees the consequences of a particular action through critical examination, there is wisdom. The critical thought process is the flip side of the creativity coin. Both sides are essential—assuming you want success.

Rigorous examination can be self-defeating if the wrong question is asked. The right question is, How do we make these strategies work? Or, What would it take to improve this approach so that success is guaranteed? The wrong question is, Why will these strategies not work? Evaluation identifies weaknesses and consequences of goals and methods, but not with the intent of defeat. The intent is to identify the strength and ask what will make it stronger. The weak side will be clearly seen in order to make sure the weakness is addressed.

Obviously some plans or strategies are so troubled that fixing the problems becomes too complicated or risky. An old boiler that has some leaks (shortcomings in a plan) can be patched, plugged, and mended in order to heat the water needed. If all that fixing results in a blowout, a whole new approach that includes throwing the old boiler away is the best plan. The most essential step in critical thinking is to structure the time to do it well. Test and retest the model. Strong models will prevail. The toolbox in chapter 8 provides a few suggestions for enhancing the critical analysis skills in teams.

Teams need creativity and critical analysis to be successful. The cocreation notion and rigorous consequential thinking of the wisdom literature provides a theological basis for ministry teams to excel.

The Spiritual Practice of Habits

A spiritual habit of virtue is a consistent practice that brings about spiritual transformation. Practices of kindness produce a kind soul. Great athletes or surgeons implement disciplined practice of skills that bring mastery to their crafts. Creativity, critical thinking, implementation, and team meeting management all benefit when team members develop their crafts. The concept is simple; the implementation is perceived as hard.

How do spiritual habits bring spiritual maturity? How do spiritual habits impact the work of teams? Practice of certain habits brings change in character in ways similar to the improvements observed in skills. More precisely, those practices place us in a position where transformation occurs through grace—more about that later.

One of the "hard sayings" of Jesus is the suggestion in Matthew 5:27–30 and Matthew 18:7–9 to cut off your hand if it is leading you to sin, because it is better to go into heaven with only one hand than to miss heaven altogether because you could not avoid the sin. There have been weirdos in church history that took the words literally rather than understand the metaphor that Jesus spoke. The mystery of "cut off your hand" is resolved when you understand two principles.

Principle number one is that final goals are the ultimate reality. Jesus was saying, keep the important stuff important—keep the main things the main thing. Do whatever it takes to get to the important things. If someone was going to give you a life that would not end (immortality), would it not be worth doing something extreme (like cutting off your hand)?

Principle number two is that *the will* is the secret to creating the behaviors that will enable you to pursue spiritual goals. If I handed you a knife and said, "Cut off your hand," the only reasonable response would be to tell me and my crazy statement to go away. Remember the strange story of hiker Aron Ralston, who, in order to survive, cut off his arm after being trapped by a boulder in a Colorado wilderness? If you were convinced that cutting off your hand would save your life, it would take a phenomenal energizing of your will to perform what, in most instances, is considered absolutely absurd behavior. Now, if you could muster that kind of will power, then certainly you hold the minimal level of will power needed to restrain you from the bad behavior that would lead you away from eternal life.

Habits are created when small choices create action on our world. A choice of our will gives birth to a behavior, which gives birth to a habit, which gives birth to an inner transformation of our character. This cycle works both to avoid bad character and to create good character. Here is a familiar story on the bad end of the cycle. Joe is married to Martha. Joe meets a woman named Cathy at work. Cathy is attractive and likeable. Joe begins to think about this attraction, and one thought leads to choices for other thoughts. Thoughts are a behavior. Joe can imagine a sexual relationship with Cathy. Other small and "innocent" behaviors follow. Joe's character commitment to fidelity is slowly transformed. The opportunity arises. Joe betrays his marriage and maybe even surprises himself. But his character was transformed long before. He had developed a habit of unfaithfulness that changed both his inner and outer worlds. Jesus would say, "Tear out your eyeball" if it's going to lead you down this pathway. If you had the will to tear out your eye, do you not have the will to turn your head away from looking or to replace an inappropriate thought with a good thought?

The most important factor about spiritual habits is the goal. If the goal is to have undivided loyalty to my spouse, then there are habits of virtue which are put into place to achieve that end. Habits are like the scaffolding you see on the outside of a building renovation. The scaffolding is created so that the work of transformation can occur. The final product is a building of beauty with no evidence of the work scaffolding.

Habits can focus on avoiding negative behavior, and that is a helpful approach. Joe needs to choose to avoid certain things (e.g., inappropriate sexual thoughts) in order to protect his goal of personal trustworthiness. Joe also needs to choose a set of positive behaviors that will move him closer to the goal of being a person of faithfulness and loyalty. A positive habit includes finding ways to strengthen his marriage to Martha by adding words of encouragement in the relationship on a daily basis. The small choices give way to consistent behaviors (habits), which increase his resolve to be faithful (character) and find him one day being able to imagine only a life with Martha. There are a million behaviors (thoughts, actions, emotions) that can lead to spiritual transformation.

My youngest daughter came to me one day when she was in fifth grade and suggested that I give her a penny today and then each day for the next month I agree to double the number of pennies that I give her. I smiled and told her I'd be glad to agree to the deal if she would exchange each penny for a minute of time working on house projects for the next month. We both laughed, as she knew I knew the trick she was bringing to me from math class. The doubling effect or geometric growth starts with small change. From 1 to 2 to 4 to 8 cents seems like little impact, and even at two weeks I would have been out only a modest $81.92. I would have gained a full-time employee for house projects, however, with my counterproposal. At thirty days the doubling effect has taken my bill to $5,368,709 dollars—a growth effect almost beyond belief. Spiritual formation through habits does not produce growth as smoothly or significantly as geometric growth, but small beginnings do translate to big effects. Small actions compounded over time result in great impact.

A Deeper Thought about Habits of Virtue

Before leaving the discussion of habits, there is one important footnote. If character formation is simply a matter of habits, where does grace belong? Is spiritual transformation simply a mechanistic process, or a work of the Spirit of God? Repetition creates readiness, but actual transformation is a God-wired process. When a child learns to ride a bike, the muscles, coordination, and balance converge to create a learned skilled that becomes an essential part of the child. The idiom, "You never forget how to ride a bike," references that reality. Scientists believe these "sensory motor memories," sometimes called "muscle memories," are stored in the brain and people are able to access them readily after years of not riding a bike. The person may or may not remember anything about the color of the first bike or the sidewalk traveled when that initial skill was learned, because that represents a different type of memory.

Character transformation is like the *bike riding skill*. The external practice to learn to ride the bike is a mechanical skill that only provides the readiness for what the brain does to create the sensory motor memory. There is mystery as to how that brain process works, but the depth of physical learning is unmistakable. Somehow in the spiritual core of our life a similar wiring of grace occurs with spiritual disciplines. There is mystery about how a person is genuinely kinder or more faithful, yet the result is unmistakable. Just as the brain learns to ride the bike, the soul learns to endure or be kind in this moment of grace. Grace *can* transform apart from disciplined habits, as in a miraculous event. More common is the experience of transformation from a state of readiness to the practice of the spiritual habits. The spiritual learning changes the person forever.

So bring it back to teams. How does the spiritual formation principle of habits help teams? The habits process works with all the spiritual issues tied to team dimensions: power, care, energy, or getting results. For example, to achieve powerful results the team needs to "habit-ualize" several things. Make results an important focus for the team. Believe in the cocreator theology. The team must develop an ethos that says we can and should make a difference. Team members become a driving creative force that will transform the church and local community. Avoid classic attitudes that prevent church teams from being creative. Identify some habits that foster creativity, make choices to act on those behaviors, and the habits will transform your team members. Creativity is more than just a skill; it is tied to spiritual character. In the image of God we cocreate the kingdom of God.

8

The Coach's Toolbox

Tools for Achieving Results in Teams

Warning Label

Consult the coach's warning label and toolbox instruction guide at the beginning of chapter 5. Great coaches select the best tool for the specific job at hand. This toolbox chapter provides some general discussion on the major spiritual formation method of *habits of virtue* as well as specific tools directed to spiritual and functional dimensions of achieving results.

Remember the SD code stands for Skill Development, and that tool works well to develop a specific skill or introduce a technique helpful to team function. EL represents Experiential Learning, and that tool is primarily a learning event to discover how key team principles work at either a functional or spiritual level. Some EL exercises are "simulations" that point to key lessons to apply to everyday team life. Other EL exercises outline a process that works well in the mainstream of team life—the application is immediate because you are already in the midst of the issue(s) that need to be addressed.

Spiritual Formation Tools for Achieving Results
Tool # 11—The Million-Dollar Brain (SD)

Everyone knows the phrase, "million-dollar idea." Making a million dollars is not all that important compared with other life objectives, but what about developing a million-dollar brain?

Creativity at its best invents new things (the type that if sold might earn someone a million dollars). A daily activity to exercise your creativity is to turn life-perplexing situations into thinking challenges. The line is too long at the grocery store; What new idea would fix that dilemma? Lost your keys again or can't open some plastic container, graffiti is scrawled across the neighborhood? The challenge is to think creatively about solving some of these everyday events. Don't go crazy and get lost in a messianic complex trying to solve the problems of the universe, but do ask: What would fix one of those issues? What if…? Brainstorm for two minutes as you stand in that line or wait in that traffic. Write it down and file it in a paper or electronic folder. Over time this simple strategy will transform how you think and behave and ultimately who you become. Then apply that idea machine to the challenges faced on church ministry teams.

Tool # 12—*Coffee, Cream and Global Problems (SD)*

Imagine what it would be like if church people were known for their creative response to life. Part of the brand or image of Christians would be not only their compassion and service but also their creativity. Next time you are having coffee with a good friend, develop the fun habit of "solving the world's problems." Ratchet up the conversation to an exercise in creativity. Pick a big problem. Imagine a solution.

One of my favorite stories from the Nazi resistance was the creativity shown by the Danes and King Christian X regarding the planned deportation of Jews from Denmark. Though considered more fable than fact, the Danish people chose to wear a yellow star during the occupation so that the Danish Jews could not be easily ostracized and singled out for persecution. Though the story of the star is legend, it is a great symbol for how the Danish people did stand by their Jewish citizens and saved the majority of them from deportation and death. There are many stories of courageous new ideas, such as hiding an elderly Jewish woman in the "isolation ward" of a Catholic hospital for two years because the German SS soldiers were afraid to have contact with people with infectious disease. What if Christians in your city were known for both creativity and compassion? God created creativity. The natural environment teems with creativity and genius. Teams represent such a powerful opportunity to think creatively, achieve meaningful results, and change the world in which we live.

Coaching Tools for Achieving Results

Tool # 13—Decision-Making as Key Indicator of Effective Work in Team (SD)

Self-directed teams learn to monitor effective team function. Each of the four functional dimensions of team can be roughly assessed by a key indicator. What is the key indicator to show a team is "doing well" or "doing poorly" at producing results? *Decision-making effectiveness* is the indicator. Did your team just take forever to make a decision? Time is only one indicator of effectiveness, but an important marker. Was the decision collegial or full of drama? After that last decision, do you want to join a new team or stay with this one? Effective decision-making ends well.

Tough decisions remain tough decisions. When a tough decision is made, a strong team feels like it was a good process. When a competitive athlete finishes a match or game, the great athlete walks away feeling she has played her best whether win, lose or tie. A high performance team walks away from tough decisions with a similar feeling. The feeling may not be exhilaration or excitement, but at least should be a feeling of a job well done.

Final results are the ultimate indicator of effective teams. But decision-making is the continual indicator along the way to achieving results.

Tool # 14—Yes...And? (SD)

An important contributor to creativity is a supportive climate. A very helpful tool to be used in the early stage of brainstorming is teaching the team the "Yes...and?" phrase. Each suggestion by a team member is met with the "Yes...and?" phrase said aloud by the other group members. "Yes" affirms the idea suggested. The "and?" invites the team to generate the next idea.

Tool # 15—Capture and Organize Creative Ideas with Post-it® Notes (SD)

Here is a simple strategy to encourage, capture, and organize new ideas in your team. Begin a brainstorming session with a key question. For example: How can our church best serve our local community? Place the question in front of the group on a flipchart, white board, or smart board. Use sticky notes to capture all the new ideas. Hundreds of notes full of creative ideas will soon be stuck to the wall in front of the team. Tools to sort and evaluate all these new ideas are listed later.

Tool # 16—Six Thinking Hats (SD)

The six hats system by Ed DeBono is an outstanding tool for creative thinking on your team. The details of this system of thinking are outlined in his book, *The Six Thinking Hats*.[1] One great advantage of DeBono's system is that the separation of thinking hats provides a discipline for team members who have a tendency to be primarily critical and evaluative in their process of planning. The team keeps one another accountable for working within the structure of the six hats.

Tool # 17—Quick Sorts (SD)

If you have used Post-it® notes to capture the creative solutions to a problem, then use them to sort, evaluate, and make decisions.

- Draw a simple horizontal line across the board. Decide what the line means. For example, a line might represent that all ideas worth pursuing are above the line, and all ideas to be eliminated are below the line. The line could represent a classic continuum, with the best ideas to the left end of the line and the weaker ideas to the right end of the line.

  The sort process is done chaotically, with all team members moving toward the board at the same time and individually placing ideas in the correct zone. If a team member believes that an idea put below the line belongs above the line the rules allow for a team member to rescue the idea and move it again. Most team members will defer to the sticky note idea being moved. Later on, a more specific sort strategy allows for more stringent requirements.

- Be careful not to lose a great idea during consensus building. People love the familiar and the breakthrough ideas are often recognized by few. After assessing the popular trends, an invitation could be extended to any team member who really wants to bring along a low profile idea into the next round. Sometimes one coach on the staff can see potential in a leader where others do not; bringing the "idea" along allows some time to develop the raw recruit.

Tool # 18—What If? What If? What If? (SD)

Remember the three-year-old boy who keeps asking "Why? Why? Why?" in succession? One of the ways to encourage good analysis is to submit the team's ideas to the "What if…?" or "What happens if...?" question in a similar fashion. Asking the question multiple times will push the team to consider a number of potential consequences of a plan or action.

New plans will always create "unintended consequences." But many surprises represent a failure to think rigorously. Think rigorously! Ask "What happens?" to the team, the new customer, the visitor, the budget, the other teams, the safety factor, the ministries' image. Your unique situation will determine the spheres of potential consequences. Team coaches help ask the tough questions of evaluation. Remember this evaluation process is separate from the idea creation process.

Here is a short list of other questions to keep on the team coach's list for the critical analysis dimensions of planning.

- What's the driver?
- What happens if...?
- What resources will we need?
- What resources do we already have that are not being used?
- How will we assess the final outcome?
- If we can only accomplish two parts of this plan, what are those two essential outcomes we must achieve?
- Who can we ask outside our current team to help us think rigorously?
- If we had more resources, how would that change our current plan?
- What will _____ say about this program?
- Will the poor and oppressed miss us when we die?

Quick Decision Tools

The team was rigorous in its evaluation of alternatives. How does the team avoid the *too-long-discussion* to make the final decision? Central to achieving timely decisions is clarity about what decisions the team is empowered to make, what level of consensus is the norm for the team, a healthy sharing of power, and time-efficient tools to create agreement. Here are a few tools to move decisions along.

Tool # 19—The Confirming Nod (SD)

Intuitive assessment indicates a strong consensus has been building and the coach leading this part of the discussion simply asks for a sign to confirm that the group is ready for decision "X." The old raise-a-hand or all-in-favor say "Aye" is a bit old-fashioned, but it works. Or the team can create a more fun method to test for agreement. Symbols are endless. How about an "Aye, aye, Matey," or a Vulcan hand greeting if you have Trekkies on the team, or inviting team members to wag their heads up and down in a humorous nodding action to indicate agreement?

Tool # 20—One-to-Ten Votes (SD)

A vote represents a quick way to capture the state of the collective mind. Everyone picks a number between one and ten, where ten is *great option, no doubt we have a winner* and one is *bad news, no doubt a loser here*. Go around the team asking for a verbal report of the number for the key alternative in front of the group. Everyone has been heard and the quick vote indicates the level of consensus and any problems with conflict. The same vote can be done on sticky notes and quickly put on the team board for visual reporting. Post-it® note voting has the advantage of visual impact as well as providing a record if a lack of agreement pushes more discussion followed by another quick one-to-ten vote.

Tool # 21—Vote Early, Vote Often (SD)

If "one person, one vote" is a good idea wouldn't "one person, three votes" be better? In the case where many options or ideas are on the table, a multiple-votes technique is a great way to show where agreement is building. Ideas are represented as a list on flipchart paper or perhaps on Post-it® notes stuck to the team's dry erase board. Allow the team members to have multiple votes rather than one vote. My rule of thumb is that between one-quarter and one-half of the total options will determine the number of votes granted (never more than ten votes, lest we lose our democratic ideals). Nine options could warrant four votes per member. Votes could be bright-colored fun stickers placed next to each option, or a magic marker check-mark (✓) does the trick as well. There is something about everyone physically moving around to vote at the same time, plus the visual representation of the vote, which engenders a positive decision. Frequently the top option or top several options are very clear and the next step in the process can be taken.

Tips on Team Meeting Organization

Tool # 22—Meetings with Timely Purpose (SD)

Never underestimate the ability of a small group of people to underperform when in the company of one another in a religious setting. What explains this dumbing-down behavior? The primary reason is a misunderstanding that peace (translated incorrectly as the absence of conflict) is a more spiritual behavior than acting truthfully. Truth always trumps social tranquility. I am not advocating rudeness or coarse behavior. I am advocating that smart people say what they know. Other people are thinking the same truthful thought as you. Graciously speak the truth of the moment.

Spiritually healthy people speak up about what is really going on. People who sit and let meetings run amuck are like irresponsible parents who sit by and let toddlers run the world. The structural suggestions below are simple and full of common sense. Support for these principles can be found whenever spiritually healthy people are present.

- Team meetings need to *have a clearly defined purpose* that should be communicated in advance of the meeting and recapped at the beginning of the meeting. No clear purpose, cancel the meeting.
- The meeting needs to *start on time,* with no excuses or exceptions for those who would choose to be late. As the latecomer joins the meeting, no progress summary is provided, the meeting simply continues with integration of the late member.
- Meetings need to *end at a pre-set time* and leadership needs to jump on any opportunity to end a meeting early if the chance surfaces. Meeting length and frequency should be focused (e.g., 15 minutes; 29 minutes; 2 hours; one day) rather than done by tradition.
- Team members speak up when the meeting time and purpose are not on target.

Tool # 23—Team Meeting Leadership Roles (SD)

Self-directed team meetings should always involve a shared leadership principle. Sharing leadership power in a team does not preclude specific leadership roles. Primary role assignments are helpful to provide the basis of meeting organization. Rotation of roles at different meetings encourages distribution of power and adds to skill development of all team members. Small, experienced teams will need less structure than is outlined here, but new teams increase effectiveness with a well-defined structure. The four roles to assign for each meeting include: Meeting Leader, Process Coach, Notes Guy, and Timekeeper. Listed below are key duties for each role. A more detailed explanation is available at the Web site (www. spirituallyhealthyteams.com).

Meeting Leader

- Provides overall meeting leadership to achieve team meeting goals.
- Plans agenda for the meeting and distributes it in advance as meeting reminder to team members.
- Encourages shared communication and discussion
- Moves the team to decisions and action
- Confronts dysfunctional behaviors with team process
- Encourages thinking
- Keeps the meeting on purpose: starts, ends, keeps the focus on results

Process Coach

- Monitors team process to assist Meeting Leader
- Monitors team power sharing (participation/inclusion of others)
- Guards the team's contract and/or helpful/hinder list
- Debriefs meeting afterward with Meeting Leader to improve team effectiveness

Notes Guy

- Takes, reproduces, and distributes minutes for team *(electronic aides of laptops, e-mail, and/or smart boards simplify this task)*
- Notes include:
  - ~ Topics of discussion and summary of key points
  - ~ Decisions of team and any action items
  - ~ Person responsible for specific action item and any due dates
  - ~ Next meeting date and time

Timekeeper

- Assists Meeting Leader with time limits for agenda
- Monitors vitality levels and needs for breaks in longer meetings
- Monitors discussion time and alerts team with five-minute and one-minute warnings.

Tool # 24—The Death of the Deadly Report (SD)

Coaches and team leaders need to understand what meetings can do and what they should not do. Teams meet (a) to share or create information, (b) make decisions, or (c) for maintenance on a team dimension such as team climate or power sharing. The greatest meeting killer is sharing the wrong kind of information. Death by listening to reports should be reserved for filibustering politicians and long-winded preachers. A great deal of information does not need to be shared in the team meeting.

Only three types of information demand team meeting time: (a) high priority relevance to the whole team, (b) complexity that demands clarification and interaction from team members, and (c) high potential for emotional impact. Examples of meeting-worthy information sharing include: (a) a summary report of key progress toward a team result (high priority), (b) a preliminary report about different outreach strategies that the team has under consideration (high complexity), (c) the confidential staff layoff plan (high emotion). The bulk of information that needs to go to teams should be reported prior to team meeting through concise written reports, e-mail, or presentation software.

Tool # 25—The Helpful/Hinder List (SD)

The team contract is the foundational tool that pushes a team toward effectiveness. Team contracts are created as part of the startup process for a team. More discussion of the contract is found in chapter 15. Another document that can benefit a team (especially an existing team) is the helpful list and hinder list. The lists are generated by the team. Helpful items are things the team does well and which it should keep doing. Hinder items are behaviors that are a part of current team life but should be avoided. The list is reviewed periodically as an evaluation of current behaviors while meeting together.

Tool # 26—Toxic Rock (EL/SD)

Toxic Rock is an event that shows well a team's approach to creativity, evaluation, and decision-making process. Toxic Rock is an adaptation of a classic experiential education activity called Toxic Waste, among other names. This activity can be done outside or in a meeting room—though you may need to move some furniture.

Objective: To retrieve a solid rock from a circular, toxic, no-touch zone, using only those props made available. The toxic rock (approx. 8–10 inches in diameter) is placed in the center of the area and surrounded by a boundary circle approximately 13 feet in diameter.

Props: Props include one bicycle inner tube cut in half and approximately 26 inches long (no valve stem), 4–8 sections of 20 ft. thin nylon cord, one section of 40 ft. rope or other material to make the boundary circle, and one solid rock approximately 8–10 inches in diameter.

Rules: As many knots can be tied in the thin ropes or rubber sections as desired. The ropes or inner tube lengths cannot be cut. No one may enter or make contact within the toxic area outlined by the circumference rope. If a person or the rock makes contact with the toxic ground area, all progress stops, and the problem begins again from the start. A tough version of the rules requires that the team lose any prop that touches the toxic area and then begins again. Losing too many resources can make the objective impossible.

Variations: There are some interesting variations to this exercise for larger teams or multiple teams. Visit our Web site for more information.

Debrief: The team can assess achievement of objectives. Coaching questions will vary depending on the specific focus of the event for your team and the behaviors that transpired. Questions might include:

- What were the keys to your success (or failure)?
- How would you describe the sharing of power between team members?
- How would you assess the contributions made by the women on the team versus the men in the team?
- On a scale of 1–10, where 10 is evidence of one of the most creative teams on earth and 1 is a level of creativity similar to a snail, what number would you give the team?
- What facilitated the breakthrough thinking used in the final solution?
- How did the team make the decision to use the solution attempted?
- Which part of the problem-solving process seemed to be your greatest strength: ideation, evaluation, decision-making, or execution?

Seeing is believing for most of us. If you'd like to see a video preview of this event, then go to our Web site (www. spirituallyhealthyteams.com).

Tool # 27—The Almost-Infinite Circle (EL/SD)

Teaching creative thinking through experiential learning exercises is fun and a great change of pace for an ongoing team. Using exercises such the almost-infinite circle in a team meeting is a helpful way to continue skill development. Here is a "brain teaser" that demonstrates the notion that trial and error often won't get you there. Only creative thinking will get you out of a tough problem.

Objective: To separate two loosely connected individuals from a seemingly impossible, but engagingly simple, intertwinement of ropes.

Props: Two 8–10 ft. sections of thin rope for each pair in the group. Thin nylon cord works well (4 mm +/-). Have enough rope sections to create pairs throughout the team.

Rules: Tie a small loop (wrist size) in both ends of each rope section. Player one puts a loop of rope 1 over one hand and comfortably around his wrist, and then the other end-loop of rope 1 around his other wrist. Hang the second rope over the rope of player one. Player two then puts one end-loop of rope 2 over his/ her right wrist, and the other loop over his/her left wrist. This is not as complicated as it sounds.

Have the two players attempt to separate from one another without cutting the rope, untying the knots, or slipping the knotted portion off their hands. Pairs will try a similar solution again and again to no avail.

Solution: When one pair has solved the problem, the coach can decide to have them remain silent for awhile before becoming helpers, or have them help other members of the team immediately by allowing them to ask coaching questions only to the struggling pairs. Here is a word description of the solution. Take a bight (u-shaped section of rope) in the center of the partner's rope. Pass this bight under either of your wrist loops so that the bight portion is closest to your fingers. Pull the bight through with your other hand and open it to a size that will accommodate your hand. Pass the bight over your hand and pull it down and through the wrist loop. Visit our Web site for a visual demonstration of this brain-teaser (www.spirituallyhealthyteams.com).

Debrief: The team can explore the frustration and success of solving the brain-teaser. Ask team members to identify what led to success. What explains our love for repetition of action that is not working? How could other brainstorming techniques used in team meetings be brought to this physical problem? Coaching questions will vary depending on the specific focus of the event for your team and the behaviors that transpired.

9

Creating the Emotional Climate for Team

The Parable of the Fuzzy Nest

Crows have been results-driven for generations. Population estimates now stand at over 56 million in the U.S. Crows have thrived with a record growth rate among U.S. bird species, expanding in virtually every part of the country. What a success story! The production rate is everything to crows. Now, this is a story about two families of crows.

Once upon a spring time in the great northern forest, there were two families of crows: the Pyle family and the Rough family. Spring was the time for the annual perpetuation of the species: the time for new nesting, new eggs, followed by new chicks, new feedings, and all the duties required for a successful final production report in about four months. Good results start with the nest.

The Pyle family was consistently in the top 10 percent of all crow reproduction operations and the key to success was the creation of the ultimate in nesting environments. Each year the Pyle couple showed tremendous intentionality about the nest. Time to begin! The first task was the location of the nest site and the introduction of *twig technology*. The crucial twig technology carefully locked together twig upon twig. The twigs provided the structural support for the nest, locking it carefully into the crutch of the branches and providing the basic bowl shape of the nest.

The Pyle family then focused on weaving together strands of grass and a little mud to provide the base for the inside of the nest. With great intensity the Pyle family devoted consistent time to the *weaving and mudding process*. Frequently Ma Pyle would search the area for grasses while Pa Pyle would show up to weave at the nest. As the third step in creating the ultimate nesting climate, the Pyle family implemented *soft stuff technology*. The key to the soft stuff was finding it. A tuft of deer hair left on a branch, fiber from some human string, and seed pods were excellent resources collected by the Pyles. Ma Pyle would carefully integrate soft stuff into the final layers of the grass and mud to create a soft plush interior to the nest. The production cycle was ready to move forward to the next stage.

The real difference between the Pyle family of crows and the Rough family was paying attention to the process of preparation for production. The Rough family knew about the coming production cycle. They were a young team who tried to do what they could to be ready for the arrival of eggs. Spring time in the north woods has competing demands for one's time. Scavenging for food and social gathering are standard fare that all crows must maintain. Hanging out in the beauty of a warm spring day or playing with a new toy were pleasant distractions to the discipline of nest building. Everyone can appreciate the "spring fever" that the Rough family encountered.

The Rough family did achieve a fundamental structure of the nest with *twig technology,* but that was it in terms of nest preparation. The Rough family had a fundamental commitment to the production goal—to create offspring. But the lack of focus by the Roughs meant big trouble as new eggs arrived. Ma Rough dropped her eggs into the nest. Immediately one of them slipped through the opening in the twigs. Later that day one got crushed on a high impact landing from Pa Rough bringing back food. The third and fourth eggs hatched but one chick wiggled out of the bottom of the nest. Only one survivor that season made a rather embarrassing final production report.

The Pyle team, on the other hand, had a bonus year and produced five new crows to help awaken the world at sunrise. The secret was in the nest.

There is a lot to be learned from the Pyle family and the Rough family about creating a team that can really produce. Those who want to understand about teams should listen carefully to the teamwork secrets demonstrated by the Pyle crow family.

The Parable Interpretation

Team results are seen as primarily dependent on the steps of production. Create and monitor the step-by-step problem-solving process and the team will have a very successful outcome. These steps are important, but equally important is the climate or context of that team. A good nest allows the results-focused team a greater potential for success.

The Pyle family created an environment for success because they were intentional about the context of their young team. They provided a comfortable home: a functional place for the eggs to be hatched and raised. The Pyle's setting enabled the members of the team to be cared for by the construction of a unique nest. The emotional climate of a team facilitates teamwork. There are several key characteristics of a successful nest.

The *twig technology* represents a foundational *commitment to truth-telling* within a team. Without a commitment to truth, little can get done from a team standpoint. When team member relationships are not based on honesty then you end up with chaos and impossible team function.

Closely related to truth and honesty is *trust*—represented by *grass technology* in the parable. Trust is a function of consistency. The process of weaving is a consistent action that created reliable matting without holes. When a team consistently supports truth-telling and other positive behaviors, it builds trust among the team. Trust allows for risk taking. Truth and trust are reciprocal dimensions.

The third technology of the Pyle was the *soft stuff*. As teams develop over time, members should develop and maintain *basic caregiving* toward one another—"warm fuzzies," so to speak. Important levels of care are based in respect and genuine concern. Disingenuous care is meaningless. Care rests on the foundations of honesty and trustworthiness. Genuine soft stuff tells members of the team that they have unique value, effort is appreciated, forgiveness is possible, and people do matter. Spiritually healthy teams become a place you want to be.

The Rough family's lack of intentionality created a functional but less than optimal setting for their work of hatching eggs. With a commitment to honest pursuit of their goal, they did achieve *some* success. The Pyle family, on the other hand, focused on creating an emotional climate that enhanced the task at hand.

Four key dimensions create successful self-directed teams. Three have been discussed. Teams need to:

- *Share the power*, symbolized by balancing a stick
- *Achieve results*, symbolized by moving a rock
- *Tend to the emotional climate*, which is symbolized by a heart

Effective Team Dimensions

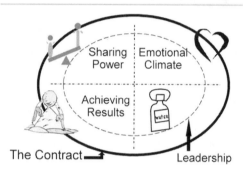

Leadership in teams involves influencing the four key processes toward sustained effectiveness. A contract is the key statement of values that define who the team can become and a simple and powerful tool to regulate the team's character and performance.

The Emotional Climate in Teams

The choice teams face is whether or not to create the behaviors that lead to a level of trust and care and that allow people to function at an optimal level. A positive emotional climate on a team significantly improves morale and motivation on the team, which in turns impacts achieving results. The positive setting enhances the process of planning.

Working together can be very challenging. The size of a team increases the complexity of the emotional climate. With such an interpersonal challenge, is a positive emotional climate possible or necessary for team success?

Imagine the physical climate represented by temperature, wind, precipitation, and relative humidity. Think of a time when you were in a very favorable outdoor climate with a comfortable temperature, gentle breeze, low humidity, and no rain. Such a summer or tropical image is associated with comfort and ease. A worker in this climate would find any task easier than the same task being performed in 20–degree temperatures with a stiff wind and blowing snow. Climate does not preclude a successful completion of the task, but a comfortable one does facilitate the task. Life is simply easier in a comfortable climate.

Is a positive emotional climate necessary for my team to achieve results? The answer is no. I once asked an Outward Bound participant what he had learned from the wilderness experience. Outward Bound expeditions require a small group of people to work together to achieve a common goal, such as climbing a mountain peak or navigating a boat. The answer surprised me: "I learned that you don't need to like members on your team in order to get things done." The student shared that his team included people who were not very likable and who had very different worldviews. In outdoor expeditions the outcomes or team goals are frequently very tangible and clear. Summiting a mountain safely is a very specific and tangible goal. On this mountaineering course, the goals of comfort from the cold and attaining a specific destination were very much in-your-face. The consequences of failure were very clear. The greater the urgency that faces the team, the less important the emotional climate may be. If fundamental survival and safety is tied to achieving the objective, the results may be achieved with very little positive regard for other team members.

We associate positive team results with positive relationships between team members. There is a stereotype that team is that feel-good experience of camaraderie. Positive feelings are not the essential test of team, nor are they a prerequisite for achieving team results. However, if the climate *is* poor, the stakes should be high to guarantee success. A high urgency goal combined with a positive emotional climate is a much better deal, but a team can get things done in a harsh climate.

Most teams find their purposes are not matters of life and death. The team goal carries a variety of motivation levels. The positive emotional climate becomes an important factor of motivation—especially for some team members. The phrase, "It's about the journey, not the destination," represents a key motivational reality for many. A team member may be more concerned about the climate and the dynamics of the team than the team's identified outcomes. Even the task-oriented team member with high commitment to the goal prefers a positive journey compared to one filled with grief and angst. Effective teams are concerned about both the journey and the destination. How we journey will impact our destination success. The more complex the goal attainment and the longer the team spends together, the more critical are issues of team climate.

The emotional climate of teams is not about creating a "feel good" climate for its own sake. Positive climate is also not primarily about creating good friendships and everyone liking each other—though that can be an outcome. There is a clear link between a positive climate in the organization and the levels of employee turnover, productivity, and investment in the ministries' goals and initiatives. Positive climate focuses on ensuring certain team values are in place that will support team member relationships and goal attainment.

Three shared values impact the climate the most: a commitment to truth-telling, trust, and acts of genuine kindness toward one another. The three values and behaviors are linked together and form a *truth-trust-kindness* triangle that creates authentic care among team members. The spiritual dimensions of this triangle will be discussed in chapter 10. The brief definition of the values is as follows.

Truth-telling means I, as a team member, tell the truth. Sounds simple enough, but is challenging to deliver. Here are some specific behaviors that demonstrate a commitment to truth.

- I share ideas openly.
- I evaluate popular team plans and unpopular team plans.
- I confess that my rushed report is not complete.
- I admit that I'm anxious about a team decision.
- I ask how the current topic relates to our agenda for the day.
- I talk about my failures as well as my successes.
- I wonder out loud how others view our team.
- I name the elephant in the room when nobody else seems to care.
- I raise the question of equity and fair share of work tasks.
- I challenge a breach of team confidentiality.

Truth is the only alternative to chaos. Truth is our best attempt to describe reality accurately. The more accurate the description the better it will be for everyone. Teams operating without the highest regard for truth become unpredictable and chaotic. The truth question for us is usually a question of risk: "Am I willing to share the truth either about our situation, myself, or about you?"

Trust is the second side of the authenticity triangle that maintains a positive climate for the team. Trust is achieved by consistency. In rock climbing, a climber has a partner who is her safety person, called a belayer. The role of the belayer is to apply a braking technique on the rope when the climber falls. If the belayer does his job correctly, the climber's fall is a very short one, as opposed to the fatal result of a long fall. The key to belaying is consistency. Performing the brake technique every other fall, or every nine out of ten falls, is simply not acceptable. Physical safety demands consistency. Relationships demand consistency as well.

Teams demand consistent truth-telling if trust is to be created and maintained. Children of alcoholics become bewildered because of the inconsistency of a parental act of kindness followed later by screaming and yelling. Team members cannot develop trust when their colleagues' behavior swings back and forth based on the proximity of the project deadline or stress levels.

Acts of genuine kindness comprise the third side of the triangle. Everyone knows kindness when they receive it. Here's a list of some team member behaviors you may have seen.

- People listen to your voice.
- Coffee refills suddenly appear at team meetings.
- Someone offers you a break from a traditional role like "flip-chart girl."
- A team meeting is rescheduled because your daughter is having a recital.
- A thank-you card arrives from a team member who recognized how much extra work those phone calls took.
- A new high-risk plan was implemented with mediocrity by a key team member and the results are terrible, but the team member's confession discovers grace and forgiveness rather than punishment.

Conflict and Positive Emotional Climate

Having a positive emotional climate has nothing to do with the absence of conflict. Conflict is an inevitable choice of people committed to being truth-tellers. Creativity creates a competition of ideas. Conflict or *creative tension* is expected. Many people associate conflict with bad things because conflict can be destructive. I prefer using the term "creative tension" in team training because of the baggage attached to the word *conflict*.

Whether war is necessary or not is an interesting ethics issue. If you justify war (conflict) because of a greater good, the damages problem remains for both winner and loser. Thus, even in "just war theory," war remains a terrible thing. In contrast to war, conflict in teams can be *good* or *bad*. What makes conflict bad is the damage to team relationships. However, team conflict can occur without extensive damage to the team members. Team conflicts around ideas and decisions should follow the following principle: protect the people but collide the ideas with reckless abandon. Create a safe competition of ideas so that the best idea wins and no one gets hurt. Live the "New Games" movement motto—"Play hard, play fair, no one gets hurt." (This movement encourages people to play cooperative games.)

Creative tension morphs into destructive conflict most often when people can't separate themselves from their ideas or the project. The psychological term for healthy separation of the two is "emotional differentiation." In theory, people and their ideas are not the same. In practice, people always attach some meaning or value to their ideas. What's important is that ideas interact and the people don't react inappropriately at spiritual and emotional levels. A healthy team functions with the authenticity triangle. A healthy team confronts unhealthy process. Truth, trust, and care will win the day.

Team leaders must remember that the key benefit of climate is to enhance the attainment of the team's goals. The authenticity triangle (truth-telling, trust building, and kindness) is foundational to the spiritually healthy climate of teams. Characteristics of team climate, such as the capacity for forgiveness and level of celebration are also important, but the authenticity triangle is required.

10

Spiritual Dimensions of a Team's Emotional Climate

A team environment in which teammates feel cared for by others will increase effectiveness, loyalty, and commitment to the ministry purpose. The list of the top ten companies to work for always includes employee ratings on the climate of the place. People want to work in a setting that values others, where trust is high, and in which creativity is encouraged. So if we want positive places, how come they are so hard to find? The secret is found at three levels. First, people need to know what fosters a great team climate (see chapter 9). Second, people need to see the clear connection between those foundational principles and the spiritual realities that guide their personal behavior as team members. What can you do to form that spiritual character in your life? Third, the leader needs to lead or coach in way that helps the team be consistent in those principles? What questions and strategies are available to keep the favorable Hawaiian breezes blowing rather than the harsh cold winds of winter?

Chapter 9 identified the foundation to the favorable team climate as the *authenticity triangle*. The spiritual question is how do we become more truthful, more trustworthy and more caring and kind? What are the spiritual dangers that discourage the development of those character traits? What are the spiritual methods that encourage those traits within us and our ministries?

POG—the Power of Group

In America there is a strong historical value known as *rugged individualism.* I believe that is an important value with many benefits. Individualism expressed theologically represents the notion that every person makes choices and is personally responsible for actions before God and men. The scriptures are filled with stories of individual moral choice, from Adam to Moses to Jesus to Paul. The other side of the coin is that we don't live in isolation, but in relationship with spouse, siblings, co-workers, and communities. Are those relationships just the setting for our individual moral choices? I, the individual in those relationships, choose to serve or be selfish, to give or to take. Morality and spiritual formation is diminished if viewed only through the lens of rugged individualism. There is no escape from individual responsibility, but spiritual life lacks full empowerment absent of interdependence. Going it alone on the long haul is not what is intended. God instituted the church and the family (and teams) because spiritual formation was never intended to be exclusively an individual enterprise. People in relationship help one another stand against the spiritual forces that seek to undermine us.

Consider this example of teamwork: Hiking in the backcountry of Alaska frequently involves crossing streams. The standard procedure with a small group is to make the crossing as a team. The team hooks up like railroad cars, with the leader balancing on ski poles and legs followed by the second person wrapping arms around the leader's waist. The three-to-five person train crosses the stream at a slight angle facing upstream. Each person helps balance the others and benefits from the deflected current of the person ahead Spiritual growth frequently depends on being connected with others, especially when the current is strong, cold, and dangerous. There is a power in the group that can help teams face spiritual challenges.

POG and Honesty

How does the power of the group (POG) help in spiritual formation? Team members and coaches contribute to the battle in several ways: by being truth tellers against self-deception, acting as supporters and encouragers, and motivating through accountability. Let's explore honesty first. Truth-telling is one of the foundational principles to the authenticity triangle. Honesty is contested at every turn in modern culture because lying has become a more normative behavior.

Why is lying so pervasive? Surveys of lying in the workplace indicate over 25 percent of employees admit to lying while performing work responsibilities.[1] Recent surveys of high school youth found that lying to a teacher sometime in the last year increased from 69 percent in 1992 to 83 percent in 2002.[2] Lest you think it is not a church issue, youth in religious schools showed no significant difference from youth in public schools. Some lie for personal gain, others out of fear of rejection or punishment, and some for self-preservation. We live in fear of telling the truth. Like the young boy who is afraid to admit he broke the vase when he threw the ball to his sister, our reluctance is about fear of punishment. Fear of punishment from a supervisor or fear of being ostracized by peers for telling the truth is real for many.

Still, lying is dangerous. "Speaking the truth in love, we will in all things grow up into him who is the Head, that is, the Christ" (Eph. 4:15). The link is clear between spiritual maturity and telling the truth. Truth-telling not only is foundational to a positive emotional climate in teams but to individual spiritual growth. The standard for truth is high. "Do not lie" made the "Top Ten" list of moral imperatives (Ex. 20:16). Paul implores us to live up to the high standard of our calling. "I urge you, then—I who am a prisoner because I serve the Lord: live a life that measures up to the standard God set when he called you" (Eph. 4:1, TEV).

No temptation to say a direct lie? That's great. What about the spin zone? Spin in American culture has become both iconic and ironic. Spin is everywhere in the media. Blame the media, but the only reason media is given authority to spin is because we work our own spin zones on a daily basis.

Spin is failure to fully disclose information in order to make the situation look good. As a professor, I hate to grade the research papers I assign—the least favorable duty of professorial life. I caught myself one day "spinning" an e-mail response. A student e-mail message asked if the research papers had been graded yet, which was entirely reasonable given the fact that they had been submitted two weeks before. I began the e-mail with, "Dear Tom: Thanks for the inquiry, the papers are not yet finished but I hope to complete them by class next week." I caught myself spinning and rewrote the e-mail to read, "Dear Tom, I have not even begun the grading of the papers, but am putting pressure on myself to complete them by class time next week. Thanks for the e-mail question—it will help with the pressure. See you then. Al."

What is the harm in spin? Spin puts you on the proverbial slippery slope and soon multiple opportunities are taken to make yourself look good, perhaps at the expense of blame on team members when the responsibility lies with you and your choices.

Every situation does not demand full disclosure, but every situation does demand full responsibility. Simplify, simplify, simplify, in the words of Thoreau. Let your yes be yes and your no be no, in the words of Jesus (Mt. 6:37). The project is done or not done. Extended explanations can lead you down the blame game trail, where you end up making excuses and end up where you do not want to be.

POG helps to keep the team free from lies and spin by asking honest questions. Perhaps you've experienced the moment in-group life when someone says something and there is a question hanging in the air. Multiple people intuitively feel something is amiss. No one asks the obvious question. Conversation moves on. The team climate has been diminished. In contrast, a solid team learns to take the risk and the power of the group reinforces that appropriate behavior.

Team members need to dump the spin and be honest with all the facts and feelings in team life. Most folks struggle more with being truthful about feelings than with facts. Don't justify withholding truth based on the guise of protecting others. Writer and psychologist John Powell clarifies the consequences of such an approach: "Most of us feel that others will not tolerate such emotional honesty in communication. We would rather defend our dishonesty on the grounds that it might hurt others, and, having rationalized our phoniness into nobility, we settle for superficial relationships."[3]

Truth-telling will propel genuine relationship. A friend of mine was in an executive leadership meeting with all the department heads for the organization. The CEO started the meeting with a routine invitation for people to check-in at a personal level. The group's habit was to share pleasant family news or departmental stories about success. As Sheri began her story she spoke of the recent devastation of her father's death and the chaos from the arrangements that only a divorced and dysfunctional family can produce. She even began to tear up at one point as she risked answering the routine question at a new level of honesty. What happened next was a new permission. Suddenly it was okay for her colleagues to express themselves at a new level of disclosure— not only about personal family stories, but more honest sharing about departmental issues.

In teams there is appropriate level of self-disclosure. Teams often exchange superficiality for meaningful relationship. The positive team climate is anchored in the authenticity triangle, where truth and honesty are essential for every team. The positive climate has a purpose beyond meaningful relationships. As noted in chapter 7, creativity is linked to a positive climate and creativity is the engine that drives effective problem solving. Truth-telling not only is a foundation to team climate but to problem solving as well.

POG and Trust and Care

The second key building block for climate is the principle of trust. Do I demonstrate trustworthiness as a team member? Trust is about keeping promises; mistrust is about breaking promises. The team expects me to be the same person yesterday, today, and tomorrow. Jesus was described like that, and the point is that you can place ultimate trust in God in every way (Heb. 13:7). Spiritually maturity is tied to trustworthiness.

Yet in teams we often tolerate inconsistency about behaviors that the group has previously agreed to uphold. Confidentiality leaks destroy trust, which in turn increases the risk of truth-telling and lowers the level of truth-telling that will occur. The POG can influence growth in trust when team members confront behaviors that are "trust-busters." Trust-busters include things such as:

- Inconsistency in speaking honestly about team process
- Leaking information considered confidential
- Missing meetings and being late
- Failure to perform on team assignments

The third key side of the climate triangle is the level of care for people in the team. Care is valuable. Do we need to justify its importance? All the commandments from the Scriptures are designed to bring good things to people (do not lie; do not take things from people; etc.). Jesus summed up all the commandments by the directive to "love your neighbor as yourself." In other words, do nothing that would cause them harm (Mt. 2:36–40). People are driven by self-preservation. When hungry, we search for food. When hurt, we seek relief from the pain. Extend this drive to more complicated notions of wanting to contribute and be valued. A team climate that fosters care, just as we would like to be cared for, is necessary.

The most basic act of kindness is listening. Listening is frequently an issue in teams. Listening requires that you put another person's story on the same level of importance as your story. Listening is more than just sitting in silence as another member of the team speaks (though that clearly is the starting point). The real test for the listener is when speakers believe they've "been heard." At the end of the day, often all we want is to know someone has heard our story.

Beyond listening, the number one behavior to create a climate of care in teams is encouragement. Move from listening and understanding team members to verbally affirming the contribution and the contributor. Think of how relatives talk to new babies. The talk is laced with affirmation—even in the face of fussing and crying. By all means, keep the baby talk out of team meeting time, but take the affirmation attitude. No greater care can be expressed in a team than encouraging its members. There is never too much genuine affirmation.

The Power of Group (POG) was introduced earlier in the chapter as a spiritual formation tool to encourage speaking truthfully. POG can be harnessed to make teams the place of encouragement and care. Encouragement will foster more encouragement; harshness will encourage more harshness. Any parent knows the importance of group influence. Wise parents do everything within their power to know about their children's groups and influence what groups they join. Why? The behavior of those groups becomes a significant influence on your children. The group behavior mediates their very character. From the early childhood playgroup to the teen social group, we want the influence to be positive, not negative. Every team will put something about communication in their team contract. One team I coached put communication in the contract, but also added two other specific communication expectations: "no whining" and "no dissing." "Dissing" is slang for no harsh words of disrespect. The fun nature of the words led to a free-spirited and comic way for the team to police their fellow members' behavior. The real victory was that the team was creating a climate of care. To seal their success, they had also contracted to be encouragers for one another. What a difference it makes in a team when put-downs are out and lift-'em-ups are in.

Words do matter, and each of us carry with us a story of harsh words—perhaps from a parent or a teacher—that did not encourage us, but rather discouraged us. The best team communication directive in Scripture is in Ephesians 4:29–32.

> Do not let any unwholesome talk come out of your mouths, but only what is helpful for building others up according to their needs, that it may benefit those who listen. And do not grieve the Holy Spirit of God, with whom you were sealed for the day of redemption. Get rid of all bitterness, rage and anger, brawling and slander, along with every form of malice. Be kind and compassionate to one another, forgiving each other, just as in Christ God forgave you.

The POG to create the climate of care should not be underestimated. Kindness changes the atmosphere in even the most difficult of situations. Bill Schiebler was in Vietnam during some of the most gruesome battles in the early war. After five months in Vietnam in 1965, only Bill and three fellow soldiers were still alive from their initial company of 186 men from the 1st Air Calvary division. I heard Bill speak in a small church in northern Wisconsin several years ago. What I remember most from his stories was the rescue of his good friend Paul Mobley.

Bill heard a distress radio call from Paul, who was trapped behind enemy lines and holding two Vietnamese prisoners. Bill responded. Upon arriving at the dry creek bed with his patrol of ten soldiers, Bill found his friend Paul and the two prisoners—one of whom had feet that were a bloody mess. His first impulse was to shoot the prisoners and return to their unit, but Mobley advised otherwise because of intelligence potential, and Bill remembered the words of his ninety-one-year-old grandfather just before Bill left for Vietnam. "Bill, I want you to be kind to the enemy prisoners you take. Remember that God loves them just as much as he loves you." At this point Bill put the injured prisoner on his back and carried him the three miles back to his unit. The prisoner started to cry softly in route and Bill encouraged him that it would be okay. Once back, the kindness Bill had shown to his enemy was replicated across his unit as the medic treated wounds and other soldiers got water and blankets. Bill said that in a combat unit, emotions and behaviors spread quickly—from fear to hatred to laughter—but in this case it was kindness. In the midst of an extreme situation with the power to produce chaos, fear, and self-preservation, kindness won the day where no one would expect it to prevail.

Team members replicate patterns with one another. The POG can work to transform individual team members, creating the team climate necessary for success. The choice of kindness and care becomes the launch point for positive team life and overruns harsh words that can have a debilitating effect on the team. The spiritual connection in creating and maintaining a caring relational environment on a team is clear. Teams must create working relationships built on the authenticity triangle of truth, trust, and care. When a team creates the best possible climate for the work at hand, both the journey and the destination will be successful.

11

The Coach's Toolbox

Creating Positive Climate for Teams

Warning Label

Consult the Coach's Warning Label and Toolbox Instruction Guide at the beginning of chapter 5. Great coaches select the best tool for the specific job at hand. Tools are resources and, thus, can be misused. This chapter provides specific tools to address the spiritual and functional dimensions of creating and maintaining positive climate in teams. A brief note on *life challenges* as spiritual formation is also included.

Remember that the SD code stands for Skill Development and the tool works well to develop a specific skill or technique necessary for team function. EL represents Experiential Learning and indicates the tool is primarily a learning event to discover how key team principles work at either a functional or spiritual level.

Tool #28—Kindness as Key Indicator of Climate (SD)

A great tool for leaders in a self-directed team is the ability to monitor team function. Positive climate is one of the four functional dimensions of team that should be monitored by team coaches. The key instrument of a favorable climate is the *authenticity triangle*. The most notable behavior in that group is *kindness*. Do people demonstrate genuine care toward one another rather than holding an egocentric viewpoint? Are comments among team members affirming and caring, or harsh and critical? Do team members show acts of kindness toward each other? Some of the tools below also can serve as climate assessment instruments.

Tools for a Positive Climate
Tool # 29—The Contract Principle (EL/SD)

The team contract is a statement of behavioral principles or aspirations that guide the group. A variety of names are used, such as covenant, charter, or agreement, but the concept is the same. A team defines expectations for what is acceptable or not acceptable. A more detailed discussion of team contract is covered in chapter 15. The contract is the single most helpful tool to encourage a positive emotional climate.

Once the team has developed a team contract, several principles will have a clear link to team climate and the authenticity triangle. The contract becomes a reference point for monitoring team climate. A simple yet effective way to engage the team around an important climate issue is a contract scorecard. Take a contract principle (or maybe the whole contract) and ask members to provide a score for the team's performance on that item. For example, the contract says members are committed to "the support and encouragement of one another." On a scale of 1 to 10, where 1 equals a really lousy job with little or no support and 10 equals an outstanding job with kudos and encouragement all around, what number would you give the team? A more elaborate format is to have each member put a number on a sticky note rather than give a verbal report of the number. Either way, the real value is the team reflection on the scorecard and determining what the team action plan should be as a follow-up.

Team Builders and Touchy-Feely Games

New teams benefit greatly from activities that help people to connect relationally. The best way to have a positive team climate is to form one in the earliest stages of team building. The following tools can be used in the team formation cycle discussed in chapter 15. But even well-established teams benefit from relationship-builder exercises as a change of pace.

Several tools are activities designed to help teams to develop working relationships. One of my colleagues "hates all that touchy-feely stuff." And yet she also understands its value to teams. As a team coach, I want teams to capture appropriate levels of sharing.

When it comes time for a group to make hard decisions, a positive emotional climate for the team, based in relationships, will be a great benefit. Games and icebreakers are ways to encourage a positive climate. Done wrong, these types of activities can seem out-of-place. Yet when done right, most people have fun taking risks and sharing. Skilled coaches assist healthy teams to maintain a balance of appropriate self-disclosure.

Spiritually healthy people share sensitive information with the right people at the right place and at the right time. Unhealthy people don't get that. Extensive personal sharing characterized by a support group or a recovery group is generally not necessary or desired in a team setting. The danger in teams is usually on the side of not sharing enough personal information. The line is not always clear. I've coached teams that err on both sides. The real determination is made by each unique team and its culture.

A meaningful level of personal sharing fits ministry projects. Part of what makes ministry teams worthwhile is the opportunity to share significant life experiences. Yet a team by definition finds its task or mission to be central, in contrast to other types of groups in the church. Appropriate self-disclosure enhances team performance. Excessive sharing diminishes the team. What are the guidelines? Here are a few tools to help strike that balance.

Tool #30—The 90-Second Autobiography (EL)

Divide the team into pairs. Announce that each team member will be given a total of 90 seconds to share with the partner his or her "complete" personal life story. Emphasize humorously, "No one can go over 90 seconds, so make sure you only hit the highlights; and, you can always take less time if you want." People will generally respond with some key stuff that falls short of the 90 seconds, but it helps people make those coincidental connections—born in the same town or state, common school, or other familiar connection.

Tool #31—Defining Moments (EL)

The team is given the following request, and each member provides a response: "Think back to your growing-up years and identify an experience at school, at home, or in the community that represents a major challenge that you overcame." This request makes a great stand-alone team conversation or could be integrated into a sequence activity such as raccoon circles (Tool # 32).

Tool #32—Raccoon Circles Routine (EL)

This variation of raccoon circles provides a physically active relationship-builder that still works well in a meeting room space, but does require a simple prop. The sequence is great as an initial team-building experience. A *raccoon circle* can be purchased from our Web site or from a local rock climbing store, though its name will be even weirder: "48-inch sewn runner made of 1 inch tubular nylon webbing." Once you have this valuable prop, you'll need an indoor or outdoor space large enough to form everyone on the team into a circle(s). Place the raccoon circle on the floor and have a team of four to eight people stand around the circle. One other important detail is appropriate dress. Women's skirts and certain parts of the activity do not go well together. Casual active-wear clothing is the best. Multiple teams (or subgroups of a large team) can do the activity simultaneously if you purchase a raccoon circle for each team.

The sequence starts with everyone holding the raccoon circle in their hands and facing one another. While the team is standing still, have the group pass the raccoon circle through their hands clockwise. Pass the circle slowly, and then as fast as possible, and create some commands, such as "fast right, fast left, stop" or "clockwise, counterclockwise, stop." When the "stop" command is shouted by the coach, tell the group that the person physically closest to the "stitched seam" needs to answer the current question. Have a list of questions and play the game until four to six questions have been addressed. Sample questions include: "When was a time when you took a significant risk? What is your favorite vacation spot and why? What is the best movie ever made and why? What is one of those most embarrassing moment stories? Who was your favorite teacher and why?" Make sure you pass the raccoon circle vigorously and playfully between each question so that the "seam" stops at a different person each time and keeps the group active.

Now take the raccoon circle and have the team use it for support as each team member leans gently backward with hands holding the circle. Make sure, of course, that no fall hazards are in your space and avoid trying this event in high places. The team will find a point of balance, at which point they are challenged to slowly sit down as a group while everyone maintains a grip on the raccoon circle. Once down, ask them to go around the circle, each answering a key question, such as: "Who is the one person who has had the greatest impact on your spiritual journey and why?" After sharing, instruct the team to stand again in unison—similar to the way they sat down a few moments before.

As groups stagger their way to success, add a fun twist to the pattern. Each team must create a "down sound" that team members make in unison as they sit, and an "up sound" everyone makes as the group stands. The team goes down (with sound) and then stands up (with sound). Tell them to go down (with sound) again and to remain seated. Throw out another significant question, such as, "When was a time as a young person or a young adult that you faced a significant life challenge? Tell us about it." After the sharing, the group returns to the standing position. The raccoon circle becomes a fun relationship builder to foster a positive team climate. There are other tricks for raccoon circles, which can be discovered in the book *Raccoon Circles* by Jim Cain and Tom Smith.[1] For tips on the leadership role of the trainer-coach to use these types of activities, check for more resources at the Web site.

Creative Ways to Maintain a Positive Climate

Tool #33—The Simple Check-in (SD)

A routine time in the team meeting can be established to check-in on personal issues or team climate issues. The routine should be visible, consistent, and viewed as important in the team meeting agenda. Here are a couple of examples. Near the end of each regular team meeting, include an evaluation measure of team climate. Keep it simple. The point is to create a door of opportunity, not a door of obligation. For example, on a scale of one to five, evaluate the level of honesty in team meetings, where one represents a winter blizzard and five is a palm-tree paradise. Each team member extends a hand, with one to five fingers pointing to the center of the table. Pay attention to significant discrepancies. If time allows at that meeting, begin discussion. If time is out, then design agenda time for the next climate reading.

During a regular check-in time ask if there are any personal events people would like to share so that the team could pray for them. Conclude the brief time of sharing with prayer. Depending on the prayer traditions of the church, mix up the prayer time format. One week a single person prays for all concerns, and another week break into dyads or trios for the time of prayer.

Tool #34—Manage Personal Sharing (SD)

Information sharing at team meetings is often a kiss of death because too much info is shared in boring formats. Personal sharing can have the same effect. A simple tool is to develop a language of time reference for personal sharing, just as in discussion and information sharing: "Please take about two minutes to share your story about a challenge you faced in your growing up years that you overcame successfully." The timekeeper in team meetings provides warnings for time-limited discussions. Use the same approach for interpersonal sharing: "You've got about one minute left to complete your conversation with your teammate." If in-depth psychotherapy can wind up personal sharing in a few moments to keep the client schedule on the hour, team sharing can embrace that practice as well: "Wish we had more time to expand our conversation, but we'll have to do that another time." People respond well to time negotiations when communication is clear.

Tool #35—Life Challenges—Why Is He on My Team, Anyway? (EL)

Chapter 2 outlines six key spiritual formation practices for use by coaches to facilitate spiritual growth in team members. Life challenges provide the crucible for real learning and frequently meet us when we least expect it. The real test of spiritual maturity and team climate is my capacity to act with truth and grace toward those I don't initially appreciate. Coaching individuals or teams around *troublemakers* is a great opportunity for growth. Jesus asked what good is it if you only like those who like you (Mt. 6:46). The test of true learning is the ability to apply a concept or skill to a complex situation as opposed to a simple situation. Difficult people are the test of your true knowledge of kindness. The real question is, do we remain open to learning and transformation as we face *the challenge,* or do we retreat to grumbling and complaining about our current hardship? Coaching conversations around life challenges allows us to reflect, understand, and choose action that will bring about change in ourselves and the team.

Tool #36—Hula Hoops and Guns for a Unique Shot with POG (SD)

Teams are often more skilled at solving problems related to matters of fact than problems tied to matters of behavior. Here's a strategy that can help bring up emotional climate behavior problems in a fun way. I coached a team that had a clear history of intense criticism and minimal affirmation. The group had committed themselves to decreasing criticism and increasing encouragement and affirmation. To help keep that commitment, the team meeting place added a few props. Several small hula hoops were suspended from the ceiling over the team meeting table. Each hoop had a dangling symbol in the middle of it of the behavior that the group wanted to encourage or wanted to discourage. For example, one hoop had a "Good Idea" sign and a "Great Work" sign. At the meeting table team members had toys like ping-pong ball guns and foam balls to throw at the icons in the hoops when good behavior was noticed. A similar hoop had a rabbit picture to remind members to avoid chasing rabbit trails that were off task and off discussion. The team had fun shooting the guns and retraining themselves in the kinds of behaviors that created a more effective team. After several months, the team had "got it," and props came down. Create a low-threat way to work with emotional behaviors that may seem threatening to confront at first.

Tool #37—Team Posters (EL)

Once a team has identified goals in their contract, such as truth-telling, risk taking, and encouragement, it is good to have visual reminders of that commitment. *A flipchart poster with key words and phrases from the contract keeps the vision before the group.* Posters made in-house or purchased can also decorate the team meeting space and encourage a positive emotional climate. Poster ideas must be consistent with team aspirations for climate. Examples could include, "The greatest sign of strength is the capacity to see your own weaknesses," or, "Short-term failure is acceptable here," or, "More minds create better ideas," or, "risk-takers welcome here," or, "Speak the truth in love." Symbolic reminders help us follow our intentions (Deut. 6:4–9).

Tool # 38—Mean Dogs and POG (SD)

Most *persons* are likeable, but some are simply mean like a junkyard dog. The practical problem is the "dog bite"—the behavior. Not to say that intimidation through growls is insignificant. People follow the same pattern. So, how do we deal with the "mean dogs" that can occasionally end up on a team and destroy team climate by their lying or harsh treatment of others? The most important question is: When will the team take the risk to talk about these hard things? Failure to take that risk can be a fatal mistake for the future of the team. The consequences of confronting the issue are rarely as deadly as the consequences of ignoring the behaviors. If one team member believes another team member has lied to her or him, then all the future decisions and interactions will be affected. So what do we do with "mean dogs"? Keeping mean-spirited people off teams through smart recruitment is ideal, but not always possible.

Remember POG (Power of Group—chapter 10). POG is a change agent through the group's modeling of positive behaviors such as encouragement and truth-telling. POG also serves to change team behavior through group authority and accountability. A group standing in solidarity has tremendous ability to change a group member's behavior. The first requirement of using POG as authority is group agreement on expectations. Accountability always presumes commitment. Second, the team must speak up and make clear what is unacceptable (e.g., lying). And third, the team member acting poorly must be confronted consistently.

12

Vitality and Energy Level
for Teams

The Parable of the Great Dog-Sled Race

A long time ago, mushers and their dog-sled teams ruled the frozen landscapes of the far north. Today, mushing is largely a sport such as the Iditarod. But over a hundred years ago there was a great race in the Yukon Territory worth millions in gold. Two men raced to settle a dispute about a gold mining claim. Henry and Ole both claimed to have discovered the same gold strike in the vast interior of the northern Yukon during the Klondike gold rush of the late 1890s.

Ole claimed to have been there first, staked the area, and sledded a day or so further up stream in pursuit of additional prizes. Upon his return Ole found Henry at the first site claiming it was his domain. Each man was adamant that he was the rightful owner of the claim. Fortunately for the story, the men put their firearms aside and agreed to a nonviolent resolution of the conflict. They agreed to have a dog-sled race from the claim site to the claim office in Dawson City. The winner of the race would have undisputed rights to the claim.

The rules were simple: start from the campsite the following day at high noon, travel the estimated five days to Dawson City, and the winning musher won the rights to the gold claim. Ole and Henry each felt confident of winning based on personal skills and belief in the strength of his dog team. Henry and Ole were equally skilled at reading the route and at handling their sleds. Winning would rest on the strength and energy of the teams.

At high noon, each wished the other well and "mush," the dogs took off and the race was on. The dogs were full of energy, pulling with great vigor and maintaining a steady but ambitious pace. As darkness approached Ole pulled over near an open stream and immediately tended to the dogs making sure they had all the water they needed and their normal portion of meat. Ole had learned his skills as a musher from a native Inuit guide, whereas Henry had been trained by an expeditionary adventurer from his native England. When Ole pulled over, Henry pushed on for perhaps another twenty minutes till darkness had fully consumed him and the team. Henry quickly rushed through the feeding, let the dogs eat snow for water, and went to bed.

Day two and three were very similar with both teams pulling well. The weather was cloudy, with no major storms, which created ideal conditions for the sleds. Henry had lengthened his lead now by perhaps an hour because Ole was willing to compromise a bit of sled time for the strange practice of a better place for the dogs to stay. Lots of water, generous food, and playful surroundings were the priority so that the team would have a restful night.

On the final day the weather had changed, with a strong wind developing. The mushing was harder for the dogs, but the wind was creating clear skies and that meant the opportunity for sledding through the night. The long hard day turned into a long and arduous night, as Ole's team closed the gap between his team and Henry's. The vitality of Ole's team was making all the difference as Ole's dogs now pulled ahead into a lead that increased with every minute. Ole reached the claim office three hours ahead and, after tending to his dogs, waited to see Henry's exhausted team pushing into the edge of town.

There is a lot to be learned from the difference between Ole's and Henry's team approach during the great race. Those who want to understand about teams should listen carefully to the teamwork secrets demonstrated by Ole's concern for the energy and vitality of his sled dogs.

The Parable Interpretation

Ole's team approach was characterized by his taking care of the team's need for rest in order to maintain vitality and energy.

All good teams will exhibit an initial enthusiasm and spirit of cooperation. Great teams balance revitalization with hard work because it is critical to optimal performance, especially on the long haul. Little pauses for laughter; relaxation; and necessary comforts of water, food, and comfortable temperature will pay dividends at the end of the day—that is, the end of the project period. There will be deadline times requiring a big push. At the big push, the team will need more than just heart and skill. Teams need vitality or energy to sustain their motivation.

Vitality is a combination of both physical and emotional factors. Water is a great symbol of vitality because of the refreshment water provides from hard work. Hydration is a key to success in all endurance athletic events. Teams function in the same way, creating higher productivity when appropriately refreshed. Explore how to keep vitality high in your team.

Four key dimensions create successful self-directed teams. Teams need to:

- *Share the power,* symbolized by balancing a stick
- *Achieve results,* symbolized by moving a rock
- *Tend to the emotional climate,* which is symbolized by a heart
- *Restore the energy and vitality,* symbolized by water

Effective Team Dimensions

Leadership in teams involves influencing the four key processes toward sustained effectiveness. A contract is the key statement of values that defines who the team can become, and is a simple and powerful tool to regulate the team's character and performance.

Team Energy and Vitality

Teams exert significant emotional, spiritual, and physical energy to get results. A number of factors contribute to team energy, including: inherent desire or passion for the team project, physical energy, commitment, responsibility, endurance, and fun. Successful teams understand all these factors to help keep energy high and achieve ambitious goals. Leadership needs to monitor energy level and provide the ingredients necessary to sustain the team's vitality. Let me briefly describe some factors that influence team drive and energy.

Let People Serve Voluntarily—Even If They Are on the Payroll

Motivation is the desire to engage in an activity or pursuit. Motivation is critical to every team endeavor. People want to do things that are consistent with their values and dreams. The greatest potential for ministry teams in the church is to allow teams to form around people's existing values and passions. Some people have an interest in working with children or youth. Others would see that only as a duty. Whenever possible, go with passion. Staff members in a ministry organization have a variety of duties and some are more motivated than others. Aligning people's work on teams with their desires pays back large dividends.

Never beg a person to be on a team unless other motivational factors exist to sustain that person's involvement. The quota system approach to recruitment in churches and ministry organizations needs to be abandoned. The quota system involves finding "whoever" to fill X number of slots on a predefined team (board, committee, etc.). Warm bodies absent of passion are a big problem on teams. Better to have a smaller team with motivation for the task then a larger team with marginal members. The quota system is compounded in many ministry organizations by requiring board (team) membership to represent specific constituency groups.

Representation is a great ideal, but adequate energy on a team is more important. Keep the representation, but not at the expense of motivation. Church structure often works against teams because there is not enough variety or flexibility to match people with their interests. Ideally, membership on a team should be where personal passion and strengths converge to pursue a worthwhile ministry goal.

Commitment and Endurance Links to Vitality

Life is never about doing only what we'd like to do. Commitment to a goal demands that we show up whether we want to be there or not. Responsibility is doing what I have to do whether I like it or not. A responsibility ethic in team members is a great asset and helps meet the energy output demand when other motivating factors might be low.

Endurance is commitment sustained over time. I show up because of my commitment to the task. I keep at the task again and again because of a personal character trait called endurance. I believe some folks are hard-wired (gifted) with a measure of perseverance. But endurance can be formed in anyone through the process of suffering to achieve a goal (Rom. 5:4). A team with high levels of commitment and endurance in its members is richly blessed, but team vitality should not depend on commitment as the solitary factor for team motivation, especially in modern American culture. Commitment combined with desire, fun, and rest creates a much more powerful mix to create energy for the team.

Once again, the importance of team formation comes to the forefront. As a team is constituted, follow these guidelines. First, search for an alignment between personal desires, values, and the team purpose. Second, look for people who already exhibit commitment and endurance. All missions have grunt work for which passion is absent. People ready to push forward in those moments make better teammates. The team experience will form additional perseverance within us all.

Laugh and Play to Enhance Team Energy

Even having members with great passion and great responsibility, the team is still at risk of low energy cycles. How do we add dimensions of fun and rest to maximize the energy and enthusiasm of the team? How do we bring laughter to the work of teams?

Let's talk about the laugh factor. My greatest experiences involving teams are made memorable in part by laughter. Why do people laugh? Researchers have several theories, but my two favorites are these. One tradition says that we laugh at truth. We recognize something that is true and we laugh because of the insight. A comedian's art is telling us stories about ourselves and others that point out something that is true. We have made a truth connection in a life experience, but rediscover it through the comedian's punch line. We laugh because we know it to be true. As we get to know people better, we have more "opportunity" to connect things and laugh at ourselves, them, and our life experiences. Teams that laugh more have deeper relational connections.

People also laugh as an expression of an innate sense of fun. Just yesterday I saw two young hawks diving rapidly as though hunting prey, but there was no prey. They were playing—just having fun and playing tag. Play is exuberance. Play is simply fun.

If someone asks if you are having fun and you need to think much to answer, then you are probably not having fun. Play and fun are characterized by a sense of freedom, full involvement (as though time is suspended—"where did the time go?"), frequently involve others, and are marked by laughter (or at least smiles).

Play does not stand in opposition to the "achieving results" characteristic of true teams. One could have a playgroup that is not a team, because there is no external objective to accomplish. But achieving results can be enhanced when team members are able to play. Play is both a cause and effect of positive relationship. Play is a fundamental need of people, and allowing playful experiences in the midst of the work of teams is a great idea. There is a clear benefit to teams derived from play's ability to foster creativity and to facilitate a positive relational climate.

Play is not the same as rest. Play can occur when we are at rest, but play can also occur in the midst of work. Rest is best viewed in opposition to work. In Genesis 2:2–3, God rested after having completed the work of creation in the first six days. Rest restores our physical bodies as well as our mental and spiritual cores. Hard work needs to be balanced with rest.

Team meetings should be intense and focused, and that will demand break times. When teams meet for extended periods of time, such as during a retreat or multi-day strategy session, the breaks will need to be longer. The big indicator of the need for rest in team life is the body language of team members. When people are energized, they lean forward with eyes focused on speakers; they look to be in what athletes call the "ready position"—ready to move left, right, jump or dive. When people are not energized, bodies lean back, torsos slouch, eyes glaze, and, in extreme cases, eyes close and people go to sleep. Low physical energy means low mental concentration and the need for a team break. Don't let the vitality level in the group swing to the extremes of boredom. Avoid boredom and malaise by making changes early. Leadership notices the shift in energy and takes action to reenergize the group. Make a decision to take a break, change an agenda item, play a game, or physically move the group. Tips on managing energy are included in the Vitality Toolbox in chapter 14.

13

Spiritual Issues for High-Energy Teams

What are the spiritual questions tied to maintaining high energy on teams? Three key questions will be considered: (1) Are teams willing to balance work and play? (2) What is the spiritual reality about matching personal passions and teamwork? (3) What does it take to be fun enough to be a good team player?

Are you ready to balance work and play? There is an interesting balance between work and play, between stress and relaxation. To strengthen a muscle in your body you need both a stress phase and a relaxation phase. As you do a workout or jog a couple miles, you exert stress on the muscle and push the muscle to a temporary state of weariness. After the muscle is pushed through exercise, the muscle will rebuild and strengthen during a relaxation phase. The principle demonstrated in physiology continues to run through our energy issues as an individual and our energy issues as a team. Work needs to be followed by rest.

Sabbath Rest

Most of us are out of balance when it comes to balancing work and rest. Both the Jewish and Christian traditions embrace the practice of Sabbath. Six days are for labor and work, and the seventh day is for rest (Ex. 20:11). A less familiar but similar principle is the sabbatical: allowing fields to work hard for six years, and then the seventh is a year of rest for the soil as it recovers and does not produce. The Year of Jubilee extends the same principle one more time to create new beginnings in a fiftieth year after forty-nine years of work and tradition. The Jubilee was intended not only as an extended time of refreshment, but a chance to correct social injustice and right the wrongs that enslaved people. Jubilee was a chance for people to break patterns of poverty and have a new beginning.

Knowing about the Sabbath principle is not the issue for leaders in the church and parachurch organizations. *Following* the Sabbath is the challenge. Listen to the words of Jesus in Matthew 11: 28–30, "Come to me, all you who are weary and burdened, and I will give you rest. Take my yoke upon you and learn from me, for I am gentle and humble in heart, and you will find rest for your souls. For my yoke is easy and my burden is light." Certainly Jesus was speaking beyond the physical rest of Sabbath, to a rest of the heart and soul. Physical recovery is clear, but the Sabbath was designed to rest our spirits as well as our bodies.

Team members who seem to work too much and play too little come in at least two varieties: some are suffering from a distorted view of self (unbalanced self-esteem) and some are confused about calling and a theology of play. Jesus practiced what he preached as he intentionally sought rest for himself and his disciples. Our work in ministry is important and demanding, but work without rest is a clear sign of an unbalanced self-perception. A healthy person with a balanced self-esteem knows his or her capabilities, strengths, and weaknesses. A quiet confidence results from accepting who I am with both my warts and my wows. People with a low view of self are frequently caught in an unending drive to prove themselves to the world that surrounds them. The drive for achievement can be born of a deep need for acceptance and affirmation. These people feel they must continue to work hard to gain an approval from others that they've not learned to grant to themselves. These "people pleasers" are pushed to perform, and lose the ability to differentiate work and achievement from themselves. This damaged self-concept carries mixed-up views on the balance between work and play into the team. Teams with super achievers and workaholics find it difficult to rest and play.

At the other end of the self-esteem scale are those who are truly arrogant. Working to excess is driven by an elevated and distorted perception of actual worth and contribution to the Kingdom: "I work hard because, frankly, no one else will get it done or get it done right." Team leaders caught in this dysfunctional view of self can create an unhealthy value for the team. Their distorted value of excessive work becomes projected on others. The informal creed becomes "work to excess regardless of the cost." What is needed is a spiritual balance in team members achieved by a balanced self-confidence and a belief in the benefits of Sabbath.

The argument is compelling that the Son of God, who had the power to make a difference to everyone around him, rested in the midst of huge demands: "Then, because so many people were coming and going that they did not even have a chance to eat, he said to them, 'Come with me by yourselves to a quiet place and get some rest'" (Mk. 6:31). Notice that he did not say, "Hey, you guys go over there and rest for awhile while I stay here and keep healing people and deal with the crowds." Don't miss the work/rest balance. Team leadership identifies a need for rest.

Play Theology

Some church leaders suffer from working excessively because of a failure to live effectively with the paradox of play versus suffering. One of the keys of achieving rest and work balance is to conscientiously strengthen your belief in the legitimacy of play. A paradox is when two seemingly opposing ideas cannot be brought together into a single new idea. One dimension of the play paradox is summarized by the question: How can you *not* laugh and celebrate at the rich joy of life? Life at times is great. On our tenth anniversary, my wife took me back to a place we had stayed during our honeymoon. That evening after putting the kids to bed inside the cottage we wandered outside to sit in the whirlpool on our veranda with a view overlooking the Pacific Ocean. The sky was clear, the air temperature cool, and a lunar eclipse was in view above the horizon. "It doesn't get any better than this," we remarked as the picturesque experience unfolded before us. Play and celebration are part of the richness of life as we know it. There is something about the reckless abandonment of a toddler's hug around your neck that shouts, "Life is good!"

Holding the celebration notion of life in one hand, hold this paradoxical question in your other hand, "How can you play and laugh in the midst of such suffering and injustice?"[1] The injustice that surrounds us, and the suffering of many in this world, is stark and real. How can I work less when so much is at stake in terms of relieving people's suffering? If your ministry has meaning and there is a call to address these issues of justice and compassion, then your work is truly important. Who has time for play and celebration in the face of such a calling?

The story of the woman who anointed Jesus' head with the expensive perfume should be on the walls of all pastors and church leaders who take their call to the church to an unbalanced place (Mt. 26:6–13). I'm sure I would have groused like the rest of the disciples about the waste of money in pouring this expensive perfume on Jesus. The far-to-serious-about-life types miss the importance of unique life moments. The task of ministry teams is important, but is not intended to be all-consuming—particularly at the expense of celebration.

So, should you work or should you play? People who play to the point of irresponsibility have never embraced suffering, but stand only in their self-indulgence. People who are consumed by their zeal to fix a broken world look through distorted lenses and miss the playful world God has created. Ministry teams likewise need to find a balance between the important work of the team and the playful celebration of life. My experience in ministry teams is that in order for good teams to be great teams they need to be more fun. The irony is that fear of playing actually diminishes team energy and leads to lower productivity.

As a member of one of my favorite self-directed teams, I became known as the task master—keeping the team in marathon planning sessions. The only reason the team did not rebel from these marathon sessions was its ability to reenergize with laughter and jokes simultaneously with the serious work of planning. Over time I realized the importance of taking more breaks and restoring vitality. The team appropriately ribbed me for the change and asked "if I was feeling well." The breaks became a gateway to enjoying the overall team even more. And just as much got done as had before.

So how can you be more playful on teams? How can you live both in the seriousness of important tasks and the playfulness of rest and relaxation? Just do it—take a break when team meeting energy has dropped. Find ways to structure play even in the midst of tough times. Ernest Shackleton was an adventurer in the grand era of exploration, as European countries raced to be the first to the polar extremes of the planet. Shackleton is remembered by some today, but not because he won the grand prize of completing the first trans-Antarctica expedition. His plan to lead the first team to cross Antarctica failed at the onset as his ship the Endurance was caught in the ice off the coast on their approach. But he led one of the greatest survival epics of that era—and perhaps of all time. Not heard from for almost two years, the crew of twenty-seven were all presumed dead. They faced every hardship imaginable: surviving on the ice flow, the open sea, and barren Elephant Island. Yet not a single member of the team perished in this incredible survival story.

As you read the narrative, Shackleton emerges as a consummate leader in the story.[2] One of his clear strategies during the first long, cold winter was to keep the spirits of the men bolstered through recreation and play. Dog-sled races, soccer games, and an evening talent show were parts of the secret to maintaining the energy and morale of the expedition team. The seriousness of their task loomed before them, and the playfulness of their comrades sustained them.

Children bring us a wonderful gift about the meaning of life. They approach the world with a sense of wonder and readiness to play games just for fun. Play and games can be very purposeful, with opportunity for self-discovery or character formation. Or, play can exist just for laughter. Find some toddlers—perhaps your children, or nieces, or grandchildren—and play silly games so that you aren't taken so seriously by them or by yourself. Play so that you can recapture the value of fun for fun's sake alone. Teams can learn to enjoy games just for fun.

Story and Metaphor as Spiritual Formation

Chapter 2 outlined seven spiritual formation practices that can be used by coaches to facilitate spiritual growth in team members. Stories and metaphors are one of those major strategies.

Stories are one of the most powerful methods available because they engage our hearts and minds. A good story stays with us. Random facts and figures often float away. Here are a few tips on using story as a spiritual formation tool.

Stories come to us in print, through oral storytellers, such as preachers and teachers, and from modern media. Storytelling is both a gift and a skill. Those with the gift have a duty to develop it. Leaders without the special gift of story must develop the skill. Storytelling opportunities surface repeatedly in the life of a team. Coaches should collect a pocketful of stories that illustrate a variety of spiritual principles related to teams. Stories become part of the coach's toolbox to illustrate a key spiritual principle, reinforce a recent team discovery, or to encourage the team.

Conclusion

Teams depend on vitality to function well. Energy and vitality clearly have a strong link to physical comfort. Any team that is sleep-deprived and asked to work in a hot stuffy room will underperform, compared with the same team when well rested and in a comfortable environment. Vitality has an emotional and spiritual basis as well, and members of a team need to encourage each other to consider these important issues. Teams should believe in Sabbath and the principle that work and creation is followed by restoration. Team members can implement practices of rest so that effectiveness is enhanced by that spiritual belief and practice. Team members also need to explore the theological and emotional issues that keep them from being playful. God intends for us to embrace the playful and celebratory side of life. Playing well reflects a vital spirituality. In doing so, I become free from my obsession with achievement to prove my worth. A healthy view of myself enables me to make a stronger contribution to my team. When I can rest well, I can work well. When I'm playful, work is more enjoyable.

14

The Coach's Toolbox
Tools to Maintain Vitality

Warning Label

Consult the Coach's Warning Label and Toolbox Instruction Guide at the beginning of chapter 5. Great coaches select the best tool for the specific situation. This chapter provides specific tools to address the functional and spiritual dimensions of creating and maintaining team energy and motivation. A short note on the spiritual formation method of mystical experience is included as well. Remember the SD code stands for Skill Development. EL represents Experiential Learning. Explanations of those tool categories are found at the start of chapter 5.

Energy levels in teams go up and down. The rhythm of energy in teams varies within a meeting or work session. In addition to these short-term variations there is a more profound vitality rhythm for long-term teams which manage projects for months or a number of years. The coaching strategies and interventions address both long-term and short-term vitality issues.

Short Term Tools for Team Meetings

Tool # 39—Body Language as Key Indicator for Energy (SD)

Each functional dimension of team can be assessed by a key indicator that team leadership should monitor. The key indicator for vitality level is the body language of team members. High energy is reflected by forward lean, focused eyes, and a ready position. "Ready position" is a sports term, meaning the athlete stands in a position on his or her toes, ready to move reactively to any movement by the opposing player. Team members exhibit a toned-down version of that ready position, but the body language is the same, showing involvement and engagement. Low energy is reflected by laid-back bodies, slouching, eyes not focused on fellow team members, and distraction behaviors such as doodling or texting or looking at a laptop screen.

Tool # 40—Energy Manager (SD)

The timekeeper can also be the energy observer. When body language indicators show a drop in energy, then the energy observer calls for an intervention.

A well-practiced team can pass the energy monitor role to the full team. Frequently the team rule is anyone can do a "break check" once vitality drops. The outspoken team member briefly checks in with the team on the need to take a break. Generally team members will resonate with the initial observation (or not) and the team can negotiate what type of break is needed.

Tool # 41—Ice Breaker after the Thaw: (SD)

Ice breakers are usually activities done in the early stages of team development that help people connect with life information. Why not conduct ice breakers with an established team? Discover some interesting but perhaps unknown information about your fellow teammates. The fun in the event leads to the change of pace necessary to redirect team vitality. Here is one example of many ice breakers that can be adapted to fit established teams.

Arrange some questions on a single sheet of paper that is circulated to the team. Then discover who is the winner for each category. Here are some possible questions for people on the team: "Who has visited the most international countries? Who has received the most parking tickets (or speeding tickets or most expensive ticket) in his/her driving career? Who has lived in an international setting for more than twelve months (other than your country of origin)? Who has eaten the strangest food? Who has experienced the longest flight delay? Who moved the most times between birth and age eighteen? Who has won a food-eating contest? Who has run a marathon or other major endurance event? Who graduated from the smallest high school? Who is a cancer survivor? Who has won a food-baking contest? Who has broken the most bones in his/her body?" Need more examples? Create your own list.

Tool # 42—Stretch that Coffee Break (SD)

Need a short break just to stop the downward energy flow, but don't want to lose the group to bathrooms and water cooler conversations for fifteen minutes? Do a ninety-second stand up and stretch break. Reach for the sky. Rotate that trunk. Touch those toes. Lead the stretching like a personal trainer or just turn everyone loose. Brief it as you start: everyone is going to stand up, don't leave your work area, but stretch some weary muscles and then we are going right back at it in ninety seconds. Maybe end the stretch by having everyone turn to a teammate and say, "Hang in there—finish strong—we're just about done."

Tools for Long-Term Energy Drops

Long-term projects create a unique energy challenge. Even a high-performance team who has mastered well the art of vitality in team meetings will go through low points of enthusiasm as the hard work continues. Here are a couple of tips and tricks to help sustain energy on the long haul.

Tool # 43—Change the Routine (SD)

Research on sustaining involvement says that as skill increases and the task remains the same, boredom ensues.[1] Something that was at first challenging and therefore motivational becomes boring. Any project will lose its shine over time. Familiarity changes our view.

So what's a team to do? Change a key routine. Stay away from boring. Perhaps team meeting roles within the group have become predictable. Change the roles, even if the initial match was based on a great fit between individual gifts and the task at hand. Change an up-front role with a behind-the-scenes role. Allow people to mix and match what types of things they do. Maybe one of your key idea people could spend a session restricted to only critical evaluation thinking and the critical thinker can only brainstorm.

Other changes could include meeting time or format. Perhaps the team has settled into a weekly fifty-nine-minute meeting and could try a bi-weekly meeting for fifty-nine minutes and a shorter conference call on the alternate week for twenty-nine minutes. The changes need to be justifiable in terms of team needs and moving toward results. If the change does not work well, then make your next move.

Tool # 44—*Affirmation and Celebration of Success (SD)*

John Kotter in his book *Leading Change* identifies that small wins are imperative to moving an organization toward major change.[2] Small wins should be identified by your team and celebrated to increase team vitality as well as boosting team climate. Find those success stories. Tell them. Inspire and energize your team. Celebrate in little ways and big ways.

I worked with a team responsible for creating positive change in twenty different ministry organizations. The educational model included shared training conferences combined with custom coaching for each ministry. At the end of the first year, a celebration session was designed. Each ministry team (compromised of executive leaders and board members) wrote completed action items with magic marker on helium balloons. Different-colored balloons represented successful action in different ministry areas. Balloons were released as a symbol of thanksgiving to God and team success. The conference room became filled with festive color. Several organizations sent individuals to the microphones to share key stories of success. Ministry organizations celebrated and affirmed each other. The design team celebrated their success. Emotions were lifted just like the balloons on the ceiling of the conference room. Affirmation provides energy for the next steps. Other ideas for affirmation include:

- Write a thank-you note to each team member for a contribution made to the goal;
- Keep a success circle on the wall in the meeting room and attach a photo, e-mail, report, or something that indicates a step toward the goal;
- Hold a celebration meal or special dessert at a team meeting when a key progress marker has been surpassed;
- (*Put your great idea here*).

Spiritual Formation Tools for Maintaining Team Energy

The tools above address the functional dimensions of team energy for both the long term and short term. Foundational to those tools are the theological concepts presented in chapter 13 regarding

Sabbath and play. Here are a few tools related specifically to helping team members recreate.

Tool # 45—Personal Sabbath Rest (EL)

Encourage individual team members to integrate Sabbath into personal lifestyle. It will make you a better team member. Here are journal questions for you to consider: "Reflect on the patterns of work and rest that seem to be a good fit for your personal mission statement. How close do you come to a consistent ritual of a weekly Sabbath rest? What plan could you make to reestablish that pattern?"

Tool # 46—Search for a Story on Playing with Purpose (EL)

One of the great regrets people have often concerns life decisions made about key relationships. Given a redo, a different choice would be made. People wish they had spent more time with their sons and daughters before they graduated and left their houses. Spouses wish for time lost in the busiest cycle of life because they now realize some of those "important projects" don't look so important anymore.

Finding time to relax and play with those we really love is a big part of the work/rest balance. To avoid ending up stuck with these regrets, try the activity of "searching for story." Remember that stories inform and persuade, but they must have impact. So, write your own story about a relationship lost—the Mom you wished had been more present for you, and your commitment to be a different kind of parent. Or, find someone else's story that communicates the message. The story may be a short narrative, a poem, a music video. Listen to the story regularly. Action and transformation will flow into your life through the power of story.

Tool # 47—A Short Word about Mystical Experience (EL)

Remember that coaches should utilize the six traditional pathways to spiritual formation (chapter 2). Some Christians are not comfortable with the term mystical, creating images of New Age religions. But mystical means *having a spiritual meaning or reality that is neither apparent to the senses nor obvious to the intelligence.*[3] Mystical means that God does something that supersedes our ability to understand rationally and/or emotionally. Mystical experience defines a path of transformation with little control and yet tremendous power. God works in a manner and timing that is not controlled by our plans or habits or little toolboxes. It's a God thing.

> For he says to Moses, "I will have mercy on whom I have mercy, /and I will have compassion on whom I have compassion." It does not, therefore, depend on man's desire or effort, but on God's mercy. For the Scripture says to Pharaoh: "I raised you up for this very purpose, that I might display my power in you and that my name might be proclaimed in all the earth." Therefore God has mercy on whom he wants to have mercy, and he hardens whom he wants to harden. (Rom. 9:15–18)

Does this mean we stand passively by and adopt a deterministic view of spiritual growth, in which nothing matters? We have again stepped into that ultimate paradox of human choice and God's sovereignty, and those ideas will remain in tension. What is never in confusion is our response to the paradox. People only have the power to do something with one side of that paradox (the choice). Stand ready. Pursue God. Look for the work of grace and transformation. To attempt to focus on the other side of the paradox (sovereignty) is the attempt by man to try to be God.

The role of coaches and team members is to pursue God and attempt to close gaps through harnessing the power of story and metaphor, power of groups (POG), habits of virtue, life challenges, and reflection. On each of those pathways we are looking for the encounter with God that does transform. God is always mystery! Sometimes the experience of change will be more mystical than other times. If we pursue God with all our heart, mind, and strength (Deut. 6:4–5), God will meet us and change us.

15

Team Development
Getting the Right Start

Getting the right start is always a big deal. Relationships, business start-ups, foundations, child rearing, and everything else you want to go well in this life need good starts. As a consultant and coach for teams, there is often an invitation to me to come "fix my team." Interventions along the journey certainly help, but starting well is so much easier. Let me make some suggestions on how to develop that high-functioning team that this book has described. Important topics relating to a good start include: team purpose, recruitment, team contract, and training and development exercises.

The Team Purpose

Chapter 1 talks about the decision for an organization to use teams. Let me say it again. Team operates best in a team-based organization (TBO). Executive leadership in churches and parachurch ministries must look closely at what a team-based organization demands from a particular leader's leadership philosophy. A team approach does not work well with many leaders. Though any marriage can work with enough effort and commitment, great marriages are based on a good match—reasonably healthy people with similar world views—who then work hard and stay committed. Teams are like marriages. Teams will function best in organizations that truly want to be TBOs.

Assume you have a context in which a team is empowered to operate. The team also needs a clear purpose. The team may refine the purpose to be more specific, but the initial parameters should be clear. For example: "Our team will set the visionary agenda for this church for the next two to three years," or, "Our team will design and deliver the leadership development program for our expanding recovery groups' ministry." Purpose or vision starts broad and then is refined. Teams need that broad vision as minimal definition to get started. Teams can also be charged with a more specific purpose if the scope is already defined by the ministry: "The music ministry team will organize and train enough worship teams to lead the three different worship venues each week in addition to delivering the three special event music programs." Have a purpose and then begin to decide who should be on that team.

Team Recruitment

Recruitment issues have been raised throughout the book. To recap quickly: whenever possible, allow team members to volunteer (participating once the purpose of the team has been shared), make sure the commitments to team membership are understood in advance, and keep power-hungry snakes and mean dogs off teams.

Create diversity on the team. Insist on a value commitment and passion for the purpose and mission of the team. With that motivation as the baseline, bring on the diversity. Diversity of life experiences (which includes gender, race, age, ethnicity, etc.), temperaments, and skill sets enhance problem solving and team effectiveness.

Screening for selection should include identifying leadership potential. Self-directed teams share the leadership role, but the team benefits from members who can already demonstrate leadership skills in group settings. As the team progresses, the sharing of leadership will enhance the leadership development. Moving to self-directed teams is an important by-product of teams in a TBO.

Spiritual commitment is important, of course, but a teachable attitude must be a close second, because genuine spiritual maturity and commitment presumes a readiness to learn. As Jesus is quoted in Mark 10:15, "I tell you the truth, anyone who will not receive the kingdom of God like a little child will never enter it." Spirituality is all about being a learner. *Disciple* literally means "learner." Team effectiveness is all about learning. Initial training is part of the learning, but dealing with issues and conflicts during the team process demands openness to new learnings. At the end of the day, the important self-discovery learning may be that one's spiritual blind spot is the big problem. Fully devoted followers of Christ are passionate learners.

Exercise the gift of discernment to make the best recruitment decision. The best advice for creating a highly effective team is to spend enough time on the recruitment phase. Teams are a great place to develop spiritual leaders, yet a team without leadership and spiritual maturity in multiple members is no longer an environment to develop younger leaders. The spiritual issues identified in this book should assist churches to discover mature spiritual leaders. Huge headaches can be avoided in team effectiveness when recruitment is done well.

The Team Contract

The team contract is the most important tool to manage the effectiveness of a team and its four dimensions of power shared, emotional climate, problem solving, and vitality. A contract identifies the central characteristics of a team by determining behavioral boundaries. To identify what is most important to us defines the boundary of what is acceptable and unacceptable in terms of team member behavior. Team members are not perfect, and we can never fully realize our aspirations. But declaring our expectations for ourselves and our team is critical.

A contract is an agreement between various parties that defines the relationship. Principles in the team contract might identify some very specific behaviors, but generally embrace broader aspirations. Teams function best when core values of the team are identified, accepted, and consistently demonstrated. Core values are identified in the team contract. Respect for one another, willingness to try new things, confidentiality, and listening to one another are examples of these aspirations. An example of a specific behavior might be attendance at team meetings or financial contribution to the ministry.

Contracts go by different names in different circles. Some churches prefer to use the biblical word *covenant*. Other teams use the word *charter,* or *agreement* or *compact*. The fundamental concept is the same: a description of what we expect of one another. A long and interesting history exists in the church about groups of believers making these types of agreements with one another. Team contracts are one example of that broader tradition.

Four important principles exist for team contracts: identification of principles, buy-in, open contract, and accountability. Identification is frequently done one of two ways. A team contract can be presented to the group with traditional helpful principles, and the team discusses them and then agrees to accept, or "buy-in," to the items. Here is a list of common team commitments.

- Be fully present and involved at meetings.
- Respect one another and each other's ideas.
- Support and encourage one another.
- Listen well to others and give voice to your ideas.
- Have fun.
- Share the workload.
- Be willing to try new things.
- Be truthful.
- Contribute to a safe environment.
- Respect confidentiality on confidential matters.

An alternative approach to creating a team contract is to start with a blank white board or flipchart and have the team put together a list of principles they know to be important in having a successful team. Most self-generated lists will show remarkable consistency from team to team. I frequently opt for this approach, as it is a natural segue to the ownership or buy-in principle.

Buy-in by the group is essential. It is important that team members discuss the contract to establish an understanding of these aspirations and expectations. In Western culture, the *signature* has become the symbol of acceptance of agreement. A bit simpler, don't you think, than cultural practices such as cutting animals in half and walking between the two parts. A bit less personal than giving my word and a good hand shake. Teams may wish to sign names in the margins around the team contract or create another way to affirm the ownership of this initial covenant.

The third principle is the *open contract*. A contract is made to be amended. A team reserves the right to clarify principles. Perhaps a new principle will be added as the new team learns to work with one another. Offer an explanation for the open contract principle. Teams intuitively accept the open contract ideal. Then coaches wait for the first real-life opportunity to ask the team if an amendment is necessary.

Keep in mind, a contract ignored is a worthless piece of paper. Team contracts that are only an intellectual exercise during team building are worthless. The team must challenge behaviors that are inconsistent with the founding principles. How the challenge occurs can take many forms, but *accountability is essential*. When a team member reminds the group about a promise to listen well, that may be sufficient to adjust behavior. The team's behavior may be so far from original expectations that a more stringent intervention will be necessary. For example, the "magic stick" is an old tool that forces team members to listen to one another, because a person can only talk when holding the stick (or ball, or magic pen, or etc.). I learned that tool as a children's game to develop social skills, but have used it for several adult groups to get behavior back on track.

Accountability is the real heart of team contracts. People want to be truthful and kind and respectful, but no one lives out those values all the time. When I commit myself to follow those values, I make a major step to model those behaviors as a team member. When I stand with a group of people who have also committed to those values, I will walk my talk more consistently. When I fall short and people encourage me to be more consistent, that also works to my favor.

The reason the contract is the single most important tool in team effectiveness is because it sets an expectation for team function *and* it pulls us forward to achieve those expectations. Contract principles will spread across the four functional dimensions of team: power, care, results, and fun. Because of that contract breadth, it can be used as a quick tool to assess most of the functional dimensions. Checking in on the contract is a simple tool to assess overall team satisfaction with team life. Members share their assessment; discussion leads to a team action plan.

Early Team Building—The First Team Gathering

The team should set aside several hours of time for its initial gathering. (A day or longer in a retreat setting is even more helpful.) The team meeting should include a well-designed process to help the team create a contract, discuss its purpose, take early steps to develop a positive climate, and do training in team functions. The specific design of this process should be done by a team coach. The initial training may be done by trained coaches, who form the nucleus for the self-directed team structure. Organizations who are new to teams should invest in an external coach and trainer who can guide them into a successful team experience.

Leadership development for their newly formed teams is absolutely necessary. The principles and tools provided in this book form the curriculum outline for that team training. If the ministry organization has a vision to become team-based and produce self-directed teams, the need for external training is clear. The great payout for this approach is that the organization becomes empowered over time. Implementing a coach-based approach to leadership development and the creation of true self-directed teams enables unlimited growth in teams and their marvelous results. Pastors and executive leaders can find additional support for training programs at our ministry Web site www. spirituallyhealthyteams.com.

Blessings on your journey into the wonderful world of teams!

Notes

Chapter 1: The Power of Self-directed Teams

[1]Rebecca Barnes and Linda Lowry, "Special Report: The American Church in Crisis," *Outreach* (May/June 2006).

[2]Joseph Bottum, "The Death of Protestant America: A Political Theory of the Protestant Mainline," *First Things* (August/September 2008).

[3]Edward H. Hammett, *Spiritual Leadership in a Secular Age: Building Bridges Instead of Barriers* (St. Louis: Lake Hickory Resources, 2005).

[4]Lyle Schaller, *Small Congregation, Big Potential* (Nashville: Abingdon Press, 2003).

[5]Dean R. Hoge and Jacqueline E. Wenger, *Pastors in Transition* (Grand Rapids: Eerdmans, 2005).

[6]Paul D. Borden, *Hit the Bullseye: How Denominations Can Aim Congregations at the Mission Field* (Nashville: Abingdon Press, 2003).

Chapter 2: How to Create Spiritually Transformed Teams

[1]Jane Creswell, *Christ-Centered Coaching* (St. Louis: Lake Hickory Resources, 2006).

Chapter 3: Sharing Power in Teams

[1]William Glasser, *Choice Theory: A New Psychology of Personal Freedom* (New York: Harper Paperbacks, 1999).

Chapter 4: Spiritual Issues of Shared Power in Teams

[1]Edward DeBono, *The Six Thinking Hats*, 2d ed. (Boston: Little Brown, 1985, 1999).

[2]Walter C. Wright, *Don't Step on the Rope* (Carlisle, U.K.: Authentic, 2005). Wright uses the example of expeditionary teams for insight on a number of team and leadership issues.

Chapter 5: The Coach's Toolbox: Power Tools to Encourage Sharing Power

[1]Dietrich Bonhoeffer, *Life Together: The Classic Exploration of Faith in Community* (1954; reprint, New York: Harper One, 1978).

[2]Thomas Merton, *Contemplative Prayer* (New York: Doubleday, 1971), 39.

[3]Mary or Joe or any other first name used in the book as an example or a story character has a clear link to a real person/event or amalgamation of real events, but the name has been changed.

Chapter 6: Achieving Results in Teams

[1]Edward DeBono, *The Six Thinking Hats,* 2d ed. (Boston: Little Brown, 1985, 1999).

Chapter 7: Spiritual Issues of Moving the Rock

[1]According to the U.S. Labor Department (http://www.bls.gov/TUS) the average American adult watches TV about three hours per day, which adds up to twenty-one hours a week and more than a thousand hours a year. So getting rid of the TV time drain would be a good thing for many ministry team members.

Chapter 8: The Coach's Toolbox: Tools for Achieving Results in Teams

[1]Edward DeBono, *The Six Thinking Hats,* 2d ed. (Boston: Little Brown, 1985, 1999).

Chapter 10: Spiritual Dimensions of a Team's Emotional Climate

[1]Ethics Resource Center, *National Business Ethics Survey,* http://www.ethics.org.

[2]Josephson Institute, *Report Card on the Ethics of American Youth,* http://www.charactercounts.org.

[3]John Powell, *Why Am I Afraid to Tell You Who I Am?* (Notre Dame, Ind.: Thomas More, 1995).

Chapter 11: The Coach's Toolbox: Creating Positive Climates for Teams

[1]Jim Cain and Tom Smith, *The Book of Raccoon Circles* (Dubuque, Iowa: Kendall Hunt, 2006).

Chapter 13: Spiritual Issues for High-Energy Teams

[1]Jurgen Moltmann, *A Theology of Play* (New York: Harpers, 1972). This paradox notion of play comes from Moltmann's introductory chapter.

[2]See, for example, Ernest Shackleton, *South: The story of Shackleton's 1914–17 Expedition* (London: Century Publishing, 1982).

Chapter 14: The Coach's Toolbox: Tools to Maintain Vitality

[1]Mihaly Csikszentmihaly, *Finding Flow: The Psychology of Engagement with Everyday Life* (New York: Basic Books, 1998).

[2]John P. Kotter, *Leading Change* (Boston: Harvard Business School Press, 1996).

[3]*Merriam-Webster Online Dictionary,* http://www.merriam-webster.com.